W9-ADJ-472

OTHER BOOKS BY REBECCA C. JONES

NOVELS

The Germy Blew It series

Germy Blew It

Germy Blew It—Again!

Germy Blew the Bugle

Germy in Charge

Madeline and the Great (Old) Escape Artist

Angie and Me

The Believers

PICTURE BOOKS

Great-Aunt Martha

Matthew and Tilly

Down at the Bottom of the Deep Dark Sea

The Biggest, Meanest, Ugliest Dog in the Whole Wide World

The Biggest (and Best) Flag That Ever Flew

I Am Not Afraid

The

President

Has

Been

Shot!

The President Has Been Shot!

TRUE STORIES OF THE ATTACKS ON TEN U.S. PRESIDENTS

Rebecca C. Jones

DUTTON CHILDREN'S BOOKS ■ NEW YORK

For Chris,

who endures

■

Text copyright © 1996 by Rebecca C. Jones

Photo credits: p. 3, p. 4 (details on pp. i, 1, and 3), pp. 7, 21, 29, 32, 34, 38, 40, 46 (detail on p. 38), pp. 50, 52, 57, 59, 64, 66 (detail on p. 57), p. 69, p. 76 (three small inset photos), p. 77, p. 84 (inset), p. 111 (two small inset photos) courtesy of the Library of Congress; p. 22 (Identification No. 904), p. 24 (Identification No. 9A) courtesy of the Lincoln Museum, Fort Wayne, Indiana; p. 79 courtesy of the Franklin D. Roosevelt Library; p. 83 (detail on p. 76), pp. 120, 121, 124 courtesy of the D.C. Public Library, copyright by *The Washington Post*; p. 88 (detail on p. 84) courtesy of the National Archives, Warren Commission Records; p. 92 Cecil Stoughton, the John Fitzgerald Kennedy Library; p. 100 Cecil Stoughton, the Lyndon Baines Johnson Library collection; pp. 104, 105 courtesy of *Look* magazine, the John Fitzgerald Kennedy Library; p. 102 (details on cover and title page) courtesy of Bob Jackson, copyright 1963 by Bob Jackson; pp. 112, 114 courtesy of the Gerald R. Ford Library; p. 119 courtesy of AP/Wide World Photos.

CIP Data is available.

Published in the United States by Dutton Children's Books,
a division of Penguin Books USA Inc.
375 Hudson Street, New York, New York 10014

Designed by Amy Berniker

Printed in USA
First Edition
ISBN 0-525-45333-4
10 9 8 7 6 5 4 3 2 1

ACKNOWLEDGMENTS

It's impossible to name everyone who's opened doors, answered questions, located photographs, and offered encouragement. A few people, though, stand out in their kindness: Brent Ashabranner and Ann Tobias, the Children's Book Guild of Washington, D.C.; William Bingman, Frostburg State University, Frostburg, Maryland; Steve Branch, the Ronald Reagan Library, Simi Valley, California; Donna Bryant, Burtonsville Elementary School, Burtonsville, Maryland; Loretta Castaldi and Timothy Curtis, the Broadmoor, Washington, D.C.; Ruth Cook, now retired from the Lincoln Museum, Fort Wayne, Indiana; John Cummings, the Nimitz Library at the U.S. Naval Academy, Annapolis, Maryland; Deborah Evans and Mary Ison, the Library of Congress, Washington, D.C.; Allan Goodrich, the John Fitzgerald Kennedy Library, Boston, Massachusetts; Kenneth G. Hafeli, the Gerald R. Ford Library, Ann Arbor, Michigan; Suzanne Lander, Lucia Monfried, and Meredith Mundy Wasinger, Dutton Children's Books; Mark Renovitch, the Franklin D. Roosevelt Library, Hyde Park, New York; E. Phillip Scott, the Lyndon Baines Johnson Library, Austin, Texas; Mary C. Ternes, the District of Columbia Public Library; Pauline Testerman, the Harry S. Truman Library, Independence, Missouri; Steven D. Tilley, the National Archives, College Park, Maryland; George Tonkin, Theodore Roosevelt's boyhood home, New York; Paula Vogel, Wide World Photos, New York.   R.C.J.

Contents

The

President

Has

Been

Shot!

Andrew Jackson

"There is nothing but madness in all this."
JOHN TYLER

RICHARD LAWRENCE stood nervously in the rotunda of the U.S. Capitol building on January 30, 1835. He patted the guns in his pocket and waited.

The rotunda was crowded with people hoping to see Andrew Jackson, the eighth president of the United States. President Jackson normally worked and lived in the White House, but he had come to the Capitol that day to attend the funeral of a congressman.

When President Jackson finally entered the rotunda, almost

■ Two guns misfired when Richard Lawrence tried to shoot Andrew Jackson.

everyone stepped back to make way for him. But Richard Lawrence moved forward, pulled out a pistol, and squeezed the trigger.

An explosion rang out, but no bullet left the gun; it had misfired.

An old soldier with a quick temper, President Jackson raised his walking cane and lunged at Lawrence. But the young man was fast. He dropped the pistol and pulled out another one, already cocked and ready to fire. Just inches away from the president's heart, Lawrence again squeezed the trigger. This gun misfired, too.

Several men—including Congressman Davy Crockett of Tennessee—jumped on Lawrence and wrestled him to the floor. President Jackson kept swinging his cane until his aides pulled him away and rushed him back to the White House.

The president was safe, but the country was shaken by the attack. Many people—including Andrew Jackson himself—saw his survival as nothing less than a miracle. A firearms expert figured the odds against two misfires in a row were about 125,000 to 1.

The miracle was so astounding that some people later wondered if the president had planned the attack himself to increase his popularity. But that was probably just a rumor.

Since then, every president has received threats on his life. Ten presidents, including Andrew Jackson, have been attacked by someone with a gun, intent on killing them. Four presidents have died, and one was seriously injured.

After each attack, the people who guarded the president tightened security and tried to figure out why someone would do such an evil thing.

Often the reasons didn't make sense. Richard Lawrence, for instance, said he was the rightful heir to the British throne, and he wanted to punish President Jackson for killing his father three years before. But the police soon learned Lawrence was an unemployed housepainter—not a crown prince—and his father had died, without any help from Andrew Jackson, twelve years earlier.

"There is nothing but madness in all this," said John Tyler, then a senator from Virginia. A jury evidently agreed. Lawrence was found not guilty of attempted murder because he was "under the influence of insanity." He spent the rest of his life in an asylum.

Other assassins (and would-be assassins) offered reasons just as puzzling. One shooter hoped killing the president would help him get a good job with the government. Another wanted to impress a movie star. Yet another said she had no idea why she pulled out a gun.

But some attackers—perhaps the most dangerous ones—knew exactly what they were doing and why. They wanted to change the country forever. And sometimes they did.

Abraham Lincoln

"Now he belongs to the ages."
SECRETARY OF WAR EDWIN STANTON

ALMOST FROM the moment Abraham Lincoln was elected president, people began plotting to kill him. A murder plot even changed the way he arrived in Washington to begin his presidency.

Lincoln left his Illinois home on a rainy February morning in 1861. Almost 1,000 people gathered at the train station and cheered as he boarded a specially decorated train headed for Washington. The train was scheduled to stop in several cities for more celebrations along the way.

The last stop would be in Baltimore, where a barber was organizing some tough guys to start a street fight to distract the police. In the confusion, the barber and his friends planned to rush onto the train and stab the president-elect.

But railroad officials heard rumors of trouble and sent a detective to Baltimore to investigate. When the detective learned of the barber's plans, he rushed to meet Lincoln's train at an earlier stop. He begged the president-elect to switch to another train so he could ride through Baltimore at night without stopping.

Lincoln reluctantly agreed, and newspapers later made fun of him for "sneaking" into Washington at night. One reporter even described an elaborate disguise Lincoln had worn—but all he had changed was his hat.

The newspaper stories embarrassed Mr. Lincoln. He felt he had made a mistake by following the detective's advice. He said he didn't like "stealing into [Washington] like a thief in the night," and he vowed he would never again change his plans for the sake of safety.

He kept his promise. Over the next four years, he received more than 10,000 death threats. He kept some of them in an envelope marked *Assassinations* in his desk, but he never again changed his plans to avoid danger.

Why did so many people want to kill Abraham Lincoln? Today he is considered one of our most beloved presidents. But in the 1860s, many people hated him intensely; they blamed him for the terrible Civil War that raged between the Northern and Southern states.

The war began shortly after President Lincoln took the oath of office. He insisted the purpose of the war was to preserve the Union. (Eleven Southern states had broken away from the Union to form a new country—the Confederate States of America—where they could make their own laws.) But many Northerners thought or hoped the real reason for the war was to abolish slavery. Those eleven states in the Confederacy—and four others that stayed in the Union—allowed slavery.

Almost no one expected the war to last more than a few weeks or maybe a few months. The Union supporters felt confident because they had more soldiers and more money, but the Confederates had confidence in their military leaders and their grit. So the war raged on for four years. Almost 500,000 Americans died, creating this grisly record: More Americans died in the Civil War than in all other wars combined.

Many people turned their grief and anger into an intense loathing of Abraham Lincoln. The president was especially unpopular in Maryland, a slave state just a few miles from the White House. When President Lincoln realized that the Maryland legislature was going to vote to join the Confederacy, he sent Union troops to the state capitol in Annapolis to arrest some legislators and keep them from voting.

That kind of bold action helped save the Union—and, ultimately, helped free the slaves. But it made some people hate President Lincoln all the more. Rumors of assassination plots flew around Washington, and the president's advisers urged him to be careful. Secretary of War Edwin Stanton ordered special guards for the president and cautioned him to stay away from crowds. But President Lincoln continued to take walks and carriage rides around the city, and he often enjoyed an evening out at a local theater.

He probably needed these diversions to escape the public anguish of war and the private anguish in his own family. The Lincolns' eleven-year-old son, Will, died at the White House in 1862 of typhoid fever, and Mrs. Lincoln—already tortured by the death of another son back in Illinois and the separation from her Southern family—could not be consoled.

The president grieved for Will, too, but he continued to lead the Union in war. He was riding to the Soldiers' Home near the edge of Washington one afternoon when a bullet whizzed through his top hat. President Lincoln was not hurt, but Secretary of War Stanton added more carriages—as decoys, so an assassin wouldn't know which carriage was the president's.

President Lincoln still refused to change his schedule, and he continued to leave the safety of the White House daily. He understood the risks he was taking and spoke of assassination frequently. One afternoon he told a guard: "I have perfect confidence in those who are around me—in every one of you. I know no one could do it and get away with it. But if it is to be done, it is impossible to prevent it."

In early 1865, as the war was ending, he told friends about a dream he had had. In the dream, he heard people weeping. He wandered around the White House until he came to the East Room, where soldiers guarded a coffin.

"Who is dead in the White House?" President Lincoln asked the soldiers in his dream.

"The president," one said. "He was killed by an assassin!"

A few blocks away, someone was plotting to make that dream come true.

His name was John Wilkes Booth, and he was the youngest son in a family of famous actors. Wilkes—as he was called—envied his father's and older brother's successes and became an actor himself. He appeared in many productions but was never considered quite as good as they. Everyone agreed, though, that he was a very handsome young man. Local galleries sold his photograph to ladies who admired him.

Booth was proud of his good looks—so proud, some people said, that the fear of damaging his face kept him from fighting in the war. It certainly wasn't a lack of interest that kept him away from the battlefield. A Marylander, he hated the Union and Abraham Lincoln as fervently as any man in the Confederate army.

Washington was filled with Lincoln-haters and Confederate sympathizers in those days. (Some newspapers accused Mrs. Lincoln herself of being a Confederate spy.) Booth often visited a boardinghouse on H Street, where everyone railed against President Lincoln and the Union government. The boardinghouse was owned by a widow named Mary Surratt, whose son, John, sometimes carried secret messages to Confederates in Virginia.

As 1864 drew to a close, and it became clear the South was losing the war, Booth and John Surratt began to talk about what they could do to save the Confederacy. They knew the South was running out of soldiers. So many Confederates had been captured or killed that the South was now sending old men and young boys to battle. They thought of the thousands of captured Confederate soldiers in Northern prison camps. Imagine how these prisoners of war could help the South if they were all released!

But what would make the Union release them? Booth had an idea. He suggested kidnapping President Lincoln and then offering to trade him for captured Confederate soldiers.

It was a bold plot, but Booth convinced Surratt and five other men that it could work.

They planned to capture President Lincoln at a local theatre, then carry him, bound and gagged, through southern Maryland and across the Potomac River to Virginia. (Booth thought it would be too dangerous to cross the river in Washington, where soldiers guarded the bridges to Virginia.)

On the evening of January 18, 1865, the plotters were ready. They even had a boat waiting at the river in southern Maryland.

But President Lincoln didn't go to the theater that night. No one knew why, and the plotters wondered whether government spies had heard of their plan. They split up, then waited to see who would be arrested.

When no arrests were made, Booth and Surratt began plotting

again. This time they planned to hijack the president's carriage on the way to the Soldiers' Home outside Washington.

On the afternoon of March 20, 1865, Booth and his followers waited on horseback in a grove of trees. When they spotted an official-looking black carriage, Booth and Surratt rode alongside it, ready to grab the president.

But President Lincoln wasn't in the carriage. Maybe it was one of the decoys that Stanton had arranged. Or maybe the president had simply changed his plans again.

Booth and his followers separated once more. No arrests were made this time, either, and no one knew why.

These failed attempts worried two of the plotters—Samuel Arnold and Michael O'Laughlin—so much that they refused to listen to any more schemes. Surratt evidently became disgusted, too, and left town.

Booth still had three followers left, and he might have kept trying to kidnap Lincoln. But something happened to change his plans: The war ended.

Confederate General Robert E. Lee surrendered to Union General Ulysses S. Grant on April 9, 1865. The Confederacy had fallen. Its capital was burning, and its leaders were fleeing.

All across the North, church bells rang out with the news of victory and the joy of peace. People celebrated in the streets of New York and Chicago and Washington all day and into the night. The terrible war was over.

Of course, Booth wasn't celebrating. He knew that even if he kidnapped the president now, he would have no place to take him. It was too late to save the Confederacy.

Or was it?

Booth had one last idea, even bolder and more daring than the ones before. What if he *killed* the president?

He knew what would happen then. Vice President Andrew Johnson would become president. But what if he killed Vice President Johnson, too? And what if he killed Secretary of State William Seward? And Secretary of War Stanton? Maybe even General Grant?

If he killed all of the major Union leaders, *all at the same time,* the United States government would be thrown into such confusion that the Confederacy might have time to rise again.

Booth told his three remaining followers of his plan on April 13. Two of them—David Herold and Lewis Paine (who was also known as Lewis Powell)—were eager to do anything Booth asked. The third, George Atzerodt, didn't like the new plan. He said he had agreed to help in a kidnapping, not a killing.

But Booth told Atzerodt it was too late to back out. He had already done enough, Booth said, to be hanged.

He ordered Atzerodt to rent a room at the Kirkwood House, where the vice president was staying. Atzerodt did so, then went out to get drunk.

The next day, April 14, was Good Friday, a day normally observed in quiet, religious ways. But not this year.

The victory celebrations continued in the streets of Washington.

When Booth stopped to pick up his mail at Ford's Theatre, he heard that President Lincoln and General Grant were planning to attend that evening's performance.

Booth realized this was his chance. He went up the balcony stairs and entered the presidential box, which overlooked the stage. He sat down to watch Laura Keene and the other performers run through a rehearsal of *Our American Cousin*.

He already knew the play, almost by heart, and he recognized the line—"you sockdologizing old man trap!"—that always drew such laughter from the audience. If the play was running on time, he figured the laughter—loud enough to cover the sound of a gunshot—would fill the theater at ten-fifteen.

Booth began poking around the presidential box. He knew it would be changed before the evening performance. A partition would be removed to make the box larger, and a rocking chair would be brought in for the president's comfort. Flags and bunting would be draped around a picture of George Washington at the front of the box.

Booth noticed the lock was broken on the door to the box. And he either noticed or made a small hole in the door, which would enable him to peek inside and see the president before entering the box.

Then Booth left the theater and went back to his hotel. He checked his gun—a small brass derringer that just fit in the palm of his hand. It was a one-shot pistol and would have to be reloaded if he missed his target.

He packed a pocket compass; a gold timepiece; photographs of several girlfriends; and a long, sheathed knife. Maybe he would use the knife to kill General Grant. At the very least, it would help him overpower any presidential guards.

Booth met with his fellow plotters one more time and gave them their final assignments. With only three men left, he knew they couldn't kill all of the Union leaders. But they could kill three or four—enough to disrupt the government.

He planned to kill the president, and maybe General Grant, by himself. And he told Herold and Paine to kill Secretary of State Seward.

Booth had two reasons for keeping Herold and Paine together. First, he doubted the gentle David Herold was capable of killing anyone. And second, Booth didn't think Lewis Paine was smart enough to find Seward's house by himself. It was better to keep them together, so Herold could find the house and Paine could do the killing.

Killing Seward would be tricky because Paine would have to get into the bedroom where Seward was recovering from a carriage accident. Herold suggested that Paine pose as a messenger carrying medicine for the sick man, and Booth agreed that was a good idea.

Atzerodt was supposed to kill the vice president by himself, but Booth doubted he would do it. So Booth decided to do something that would make people think Vice President Johnson had been part of the plot to kill President Lincoln: He stopped by the vice president's hotel and left a card saying *Don't wish to disturb you. Are you at home? J. Wilkes Booth.*

Even if the vice president lived, Booth figured he would have a hard time explaining that note. And he hoped the confusion would allow the assassins to escape and give the Confederacy new life.

President Lincoln had a busy day, meeting with his cabinet, Vice President Johnson, congressional leaders, and a former slave who needed the back pay the army owed her husband.

At one meeting, General Grant said he and his wife would not be able to go to the theater that night after all. The president said he didn't feel much like going, either. But he knew Ford's Theatre had printed handbills advertising his presence, and he didn't like to disappoint people.

Late in the afternoon, President Lincoln and his wife took a carriage ride through the celebrating city. They laughed and talked about what they would do now that the war was over. When Mrs. Lincoln teased her husband about his good mood, he told her he considered this the first day of peace.

"I never felt so happy in my life," he said.

Suddenly Mrs. Lincoln was alarmed. "Don't you remember feeling just so before our little boy died?" she asked.

The president dressed that evening in the same suit he had worn at his second inauguration the month before. Then he and his wife got in the carriage for the ride to Ford's Theatre.

They stopped on H Street to pick up one of Mrs. Lincoln's friends, Clara Harris. She and her fiancé, Major Henry Rathbone, had agreed at the last minute to take the Grants' place in the presidential box.

The play had already started by the time the Lincolns and their guests arrived. When Laura Keene saw them enter the balcony door, she stopped the show so the orchestra could play "Hail to the Chief." The audience stood and cheered the president who had just won the war.

President Lincoln waved to the crowd before he sat down in a rocking chair. He told his guard, John Parker, to find a seat for himself in the audience, where he could enjoy the play. (The guard was supposed to sit right outside the president's box, where he couldn't see anything but people approaching the box.)

Parker thanked the president and found an aisle seat. After a few minutes, though, he got bored and decided to slip next door for a drink.

So no one was guarding Abraham Lincoln at nine-thirty when John Wilkes Booth rode up the alley to the stage door.

He asked a stagehand, Ned Spangler, to hold his horse. Spangler was busy, moving sets between scenes onstage, but he found someone else to take care of the horse.

Booth entered the theater and chatted with some fellow actors waiting in the wings. When he saw he was still early, he went next door to the same tavern where John Parker was drinking.

Another man at the bar recognized Booth and remembered his father. The man was drunk but raised a glass to Booth.

"You'll never be the actor your father was," he said.

Booth smiled. "When I leave the stage," he said, "I will be the most famous man in America."

He drank some whiskey and returned to the theater, this time using the front door. He joked with the ticket-taker about whether he needed a ticket—he didn't—then climbed the stairs to the balcony. He followed the narrow hallway to the presidential box.

Booth peeked through the hole in the door and spotted the president sitting in his rocking chair, with a shawl draped over his shoulders.

It was almost ten-fifteen when Booth opened the box door and stepped quietly inside. He stood silently behind the president for a moment, with his derringer aimed at the back of Lincoln's head.

Then he heard his cue—"you sockdologizing old man trap!"—and squeezed the trigger.

The audience was laughing when Abraham Lincoln slumped forward.

Mrs. Lincoln, laughing with everyone else, turned to her husband and thought for a moment that he had dozed off. Then a dark-haired stranger pushed past her.

Major Rathbone leaped from his seat and tried to stop the man. Booth slashed him with his knife. Then Booth jumped from the presidential box to the stage, eleven feet below.

Booth hadn't expected any trouble with this jump; after all, he had made even longer leaps as an actor onstage. But Rathbone grabbed at him just as he jumped, and apparently the spurs on Booth's boot caught on a flag that decorated the presidential box.

His leg twisted and broke as he landed onstage. But Booth stood up and shouted something. (Some people thought they heard "Sic semper tyrannis!"—the Virginia motto, which means "Thus always to tyrants!" But others thought he said something else or nothing at all.) Then Booth hobbled to the backstage door, climbed on his waiting horse, and rode away.

Inside the theater, Mrs. Lincoln screamed. Clara Harris called for water.

At first many people in the audience thought the commotion was part of the play. But a man in the orchestra section stood and asked, "For God's sake, what is it? What happened?"

Someone yelled, "He has shot the president!"

All over the theater, people began shouting and crying. Some tried to reach the presidential box, and others tried to run away. They spilled out of the theater and onto the street with the news that Abraham Lincoln had been shot.

Many people cried in anguish. Others whooped with joy that the tyrant was dead. A soldier reportedly shot and killed one man rejoicing over the shooting.

People began rushing into the theater, up the stairs, and to the

■ John Wilkes Booth's attack on Abraham Lincoln

presidential box. Mrs. Lincoln cried hysterically, and Major Rathbone pleaded for a doctor.

The first doctor to arrive was a twenty-three-year-old surgeon named Charles Leale, who had graduated from medical school just two weeks before. At first Dr. Leale thought the president was dead.

He wasn't breathing, and his eyes showed signs of brain damage. But the young doctor didn't see any wound.

He laid Lincoln on the floor and tore off his shirt. He had already seen Major Rathbone's knife wound, and he expected to find a similar wound on the president. But he found nothing.

Then he ran his fingers through the president's hair and found a bullet wound behind his left ear. Dr. Leale straddled his patient's

■ Booth stumbled as he landed on the stage.

hips and began moving the president's arms rhythmically, in an effort to fill his lungs with air.

President Lincoln began breathing but never regained consciousness or spoke again. Other doctors arrived, and they all agreed the president would soon die.

They did not think he could survive the carriage ride to the White House, but they wanted to take him somewhere more comfortable. Gently, they carried him down the stairs and out into the street, where soldiers cleared a way for them.

A man standing on the steps of a boardinghouse across the street called to the doctors and offered a room for the president. The man led them to a narrow back bedroom, with a bed too short for President Lincoln's long legs. The doctors had to lay him diagonally across the bed, with his feet sticking out.

The other assassinations did not go as planned. Atzerodt didn't even try to kill the vice president; he just went to a tavern and got drunk again.

Herold guided Paine to Seward's house and waited outside while Paine went in with his so-called medicine. When Seward's son refused to let Paine in his father's bedroom, Paine shot him. Then he stabbed another son and Seward's nurse before attacking the old man himself.

A servant ran screaming from the house. Herold, waiting for Paine, became frightened and galloped away.

Paine thought he had killed four men when he left the Seward house. (He hadn't. Although all were seriously injured, no one was killed.) When he couldn't find Herold and didn't know how to get out of town, he stumbled back to the Surratt boarding-house.

Abraham Lincoln lived through the night, struggling for each breath. His wife threw herself on him and was taken away. His

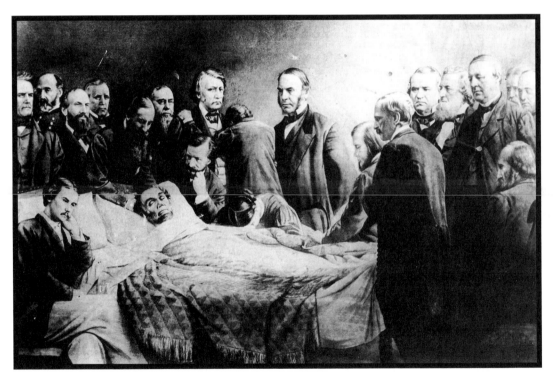

■ This deathbed scene shows everyone who visited President Lincoln during the night he lay dying. The actual room is far too small to accommodate so many people at once.

twenty-one-year-old son, Robert, arrived and stood at the head of the bed, watching. (President Lincoln's other son, twelve-year-old Tad, stayed at the White House.)

The president's cabinet members and advisers rushed to the boardinghouse. Secretary of War Stanton took charge almost immediately. When he heard that Secretary of State Seward and his sons had been stabbed, he became convinced that the Confederates were making one last, terrible effort to destroy the Union.

Stanton ordered the arrest of anyone associated with the actor who had been recognized at Ford's Theatre. Soldiers rounded up almost three hundred people in Washington that night, including Mary Surratt, her daughter Anna, and Lewis Paine, who had just arrived at their boardinghouse.

But Booth himself escaped. He crossed the Anacostia River before the soldiers knew the president had been shot and headed for southern Maryland, where the assassins were supposed to meet. Herold crossed the river, too, and caught up with Booth. They switched horses because Herold's mare looked like it would offer a smoother ride for Booth's broken leg. Then the two men rode to a tavern, where they picked up a package that Mary Surratt had left for them earlier in the day.

Riding aggravated the pain in Booth's leg, and he knew he needed a doctor. He remembered Dr. Samuel Mudd, who lived on a nearby farm Booth had once considered buying. But he hesitated. While Booth fully expected people in Virginia to greet him as a hero, he wasn't sure how Dr. Mudd would feel about the man who had shot the president of the United States. Would the doctor help him or turn him in?

When the pain in his leg became too much for him to bear, Booth decided to take a chance on Dr. Mudd. First, though, he dipped into his actor's bag of tricks to disguise himself as an old man, complete with graying beard. Then he and Herold rode up to Dr. Mudd's house.

It was around four o'clock in the morning when Herold knocked on the Mudds' door. Dr. Mudd—accustomed to middle-of-the-night calls from patients—went out and looked at the "old man's" leg. Booth kept his face turned away as Dr. Mudd and Herold helped him up the stairs to a guest bedroom. The doctor cut off Booth's boot and applied a splint to his leg.

Still in pain, Booth rested at the Mudds' farmhouse until late afternoon. Then he and Herold left.

Nobody knows whether Dr. Mudd recognized Booth. He later told a cousin about two strange men who had come to his house in the middle of the night. His cousin told government authorities, and Dr. Mudd was arrested on charges that he had helped the assassin escape.

A hushed and frightened crowd stood outside the house where Abraham Lincoln lay dying. Inside, doctors kept his wound clean and free from blood clots. Young Dr. Leale held the president's hand. He did this, he later explained, so Abraham Lincoln "would know, in his blindness, that he was in touch with humanity and had a friend."

At seven twenty-two on the morning of April 15, Abraham Lincoln died.

"Now," Secretary of War Stanton said, "he belongs to the ages."

President Lincoln's body was laid out in the East Room of the White House, just as it had been in his dream. Twenty-five thousand people filed past the coffin in one day. Then the body was taken to the Capitol, where thousands more came to pay their respects.

On April 21, a week after the president's death, a decorated train began the journey that would take his body back to Illinois. Mrs. Lincoln could not bear to go along, but thousands of people stood alongside the railroad tracks as the funeral train passed. And thousands more filed past the president's coffin when the train stopped in ten cities along the way.

Abraham Lincoln was buried near his home in Springfield on May 4, 1865. His son Will's body was brought back from Washington to be buried near his father and the other Lincoln son who had died several years before.

Booth stayed hidden for almost two weeks. Some people thought he was still in Washington, perhaps wearing one of his great disguises. Others thought he had fled to New York or Canada. But Stanton had a hunch he might have fled to southern Maryland. So he offered a

$100,000 reward and sent fifteen hundred soldiers into the Maryland countryside, looking for Booth.

The soldiers found a boy who told them about two men who had crossed the Potomac into Virginia on April 23, nine days after the shooting. From the boy's description, the men sounded like Booth and Herold.

Virginians had not welcomed Booth the way he had expected. When he tried to contact some Confederates he knew, they were horrified by what he had done. So he and Herold hid in a tobacco barn near Port Royal, Virginia.

Booth could not understand why he was so despised. "I hoped for no gain," he wrote in his diary. "I knew no private wrong. I struck for my country and that alone."

Americans had "groaned beneath [Lincoln's] tyranny and prayed for this end," he wrote, "and yet now behold the cold hands they extend to me."

The Union soldiers tracked Booth and Herold to the Port Royal barn in the early morning hours of April 27. They called for the men to surrender, but Booth said he had a bullet for every man who approached him.

The soldiers set fire to the barn, and Herold ran out to give himself up. Booth, though, rushed toward the flames and tried to put them out. Then he gathered some guns and headed for the barn door.

What happened next is unclear. A soldier—Sergeant Boston

■ After shooting Booth, soldiers dragged him from the fire.

Corbett—said he thought Booth was about to shoot, so he fired a shot. Others thought Booth shot himself.

Booth fell, and soldiers rushed in to drag him away from the flames. His last words were "Tell my mother I died for my country."

The soldiers took Booth's body back to Washington, where he

was buried beneath a prison floor. Union officers said they didn't want Southerners to find Booth's grave and turn it into a shrine. The body was later returned to Booth's family and buried in an unmarked grave next to his father's in Baltimore. A small stone at the site is still unmarked today, except for Lincoln-head pennies left by visitors.

Herold was also taken back to Washington, where hundreds of people were still in custody on suspicion of being part of the plot to murder the president of the United States. Over the next few weeks, the suspects were narrowed down to eight:

Lewis Paine, who had seriously wounded Secretary of State Seward, his sons, and his nurse;

David Herold, who had guided Paine to the Seward home and escaped with Booth;

George Atzerodt, who had failed to follow Booth's orders to kill Vice President Johnson;

Samuel Arnold and Michael O'Laughlin, who had plotted to kidnap President Lincoln and were suspected of being part of the murder conspiracy;

Ned Spangler, who had found someone to hold Booth's horse at Ford's Theatre;

Dr. Samuel Mudd, whose medical care had helped Booth escape; and

Mary Surratt, who ran the boardinghouse where the plotters had met.

Stanton and his investigators would have dearly loved to have a ninth prisoner, John Surratt. But Surratt had been in Elmira, New York, on the night of the assassination and had escaped to Canada. From there, he went to Europe, where he became a papal guard at the Vatican.

Almost from the beginning, the eight prisoners were kept separate. They were forced to wear chains on their legs to keep them from escaping and white hoods over their heads to prevent them from communicating.

Stanton declared the president's murder had been an act of war, so he refused to let the prisoners have a trial by jury. Instead, a military court composed of nine army officers heard the case.

The military trial began on May 9, five days after Abraham Lincoln was buried. The trial started behind closed doors, with no newspaper reporters present. The prisoners were not allowed to testify, and they were kept hooded and chained during the proceedings.

After a couple of weeks, though, newspapers complained so much about the secrecy of the trial that it was opened to the public. Eventually the prisoners' hoods were removed as well.

From the beginning, most attention went to Mary Surratt, the only woman on trial. Through her lawyer, her priest, and her daughter, she claimed she had known nothing of the murder plot.

But the government prosecutors did not believe her. Most of the plotters had met at her boardinghouse, they said, and Paine had re-

■ Some people thought Mary Surratt masterminded the plot to kill Abraham Lincoln, but others thought she was innocent. Other accused conspirators, from top left: John Wilkes Booth, Lewis Paine, David Herold, Michael O'Laughlin, John Surratt, Ned Spangler, Samuel Arnold, and George Atzerodt. Also accused: Dr. Samuel Mudd.

turned there after stabbing Seward. They also said she had left guns and supplies for Booth at a tavern in southern Maryland. (She claimed she hadn't known what was in the package.)

On July 6, 1865, the military officers found all of the prisoners guilty. They sentenced Ned Spangler to six years in jail. Dr. Samuel Mudd, Michael O'Laughlin, and Samuel Arnold were sentenced to life imprisonment.

David Herold, George Atzerodt, Lewis Paine, and Mary Surratt were sentenced to death. Their hangings were scheduled for the next day.

Many people thought Mrs. Surratt would be pardoned at the last minute. The government had never hanged a woman before, and not everyone was sure of her guilt.

But President Johnson—who could have granted a pardon—was convinced. Mrs. Surratt "kept the nest that hatched the egg" of the assassination, he said. Some people even thought she had master-minded everything, that Booth and the others had just followed her orders.

Other people thought she was completely innocent. They said the government really wanted her son, John Surratt, and prosecutors hoped her ordeal would make him come forward.

But John Surratt did not appear, and his mother was led to the gallows with the others. After the ropes were placed around their necks, Paine said: "Mrs. Surratt is innocent. She doesn't deserve to die with the rest of us."

But she did die. The four were hanged on July 7, 1865, less

■ This photograph shows the hanging of *(from left)* Mary Surratt, Lewis Paine, George Atzerodt, and David Herold.

than twenty-four hours after the military court had found them guilty.

Dr. Mudd and the others were originally sentenced to a prison in Albany, New York. But Secretary of War Stanton wanted them to go to a tougher prison, so he had them sent to Fort Jefferson Prison in Dry Tortugas, Florida.

A couple of years later a yellow fever epidemic swept through Dry Tortugas, and the prison doctor died. Dr. Mudd took over medical care at the prison and saved many lives. Grateful prison officials requested a pardon for him, so in 1869 Dr. Mudd returned to his farm in southern Maryland. He took Spangler and Arnold with him, but not O'Laughlin, who had died in the epidemic.

John Surratt was eventually captured and brought back to the United States. So many people had criticized the military tribunal that he was granted a regular jury trial. Surratt admitted he had been part of the kidnapping plots, but said he'd had nothing to do with the murder of Abraham Lincoln. The jury couldn't agree whether he was guilty or innocent, so he was released. For many years he traveled around the country, giving speeches about Abraham Lincoln's death.

Americans have argued for generations about whether the right people were punished for Abraham Lincoln's death. Many people—including Secretary of War Stanton—were convinced that Confederate leaders had ordered the assassination.

Others thought Stanton himself or Andrew Johnson or even Secretary of State Seward was behind the plot. Some even thought the Catholic Church was responsible—because the Surratts and several other people involved were Catholic. (Those rumors surely had more to do with people's prejudices than with the facts of the case.)

And many questioned whether John Wilkes Booth was really killed in the Port Royal barn. Fifty years after Lincoln's death, people still reported seeing Booth alive in South America and other parts of the world—even though his family and his dentist had both identified his body. As late as 1995, some distant cousins were curious enough to ask a Maryland judge for permission to dig up the body buried under the Lincoln-head pennies. But the judge refused their request.

Maybe the stories and fascination continued so long because President Lincoln's death changed America so much. Many Northerners felt they had lost a patient father, and many Southerners felt they had lost a compassionate friend—someone whose fairness would help them recover from the war and rejoin the nation in peace.

Andrew Johnson tried to carry out President Lincoln's policies, but Northern radicals didn't trust the man from Tennessee. They wanted to punish the South for the war. When they saw President Johnson standing in their way, they tried to remove him from office.

The House of Representatives voted to impeach President Johnson, and the Senate organized itself into a jury to consider whether he should be removed. Just one man's vote saved President Johnson from being forced out of office.

Although he stayed in the White House, President Johnson was severely weakened. He could not stop the Northern radicals from setting up military districts to rule the South. Many old Confederates resented the harsh treatment they received in those districts, and they took out their anger on former slaves.

That anger continued long after the war was over and the military districts were abolished. Over the next century, bitter and confused white people kept thousands of African-Americans from getting jobs, going to schools, and even using public restrooms. African-Americans were humiliated, mistreated, and sometimes even killed.

For generations, Americans told each other things would have been different if Abraham Lincoln had lived. They thought he would have brought the shattered country together with peace and fairness. His death, they said, was the final tragedy of the Civil War.

James A. Garfield

"My God, how many hours of sorrow
I have passed in this town."
ROBERT TODD LINCOLN

EVEN IN Abraham Lincoln's time, the hallways of the White House were crowded with people hoping to see the president. In the middle of the Civil War, President Lincoln opened his doors to the public for an hour or so every day and saw as many people as he could.

Some of the people, like the former slave who needed her husband's army pay, wanted the president to fix a personal problem with the government. Most, though, were looking for government jobs.

As head of the government, the president was responsible for hiring someone to fill every government position—from the customs collector in New York City to the postmaster in Warsaw, Indiana. The president generally followed the "spoils system" (based on that old saying "To the victor belong the spoils") and gave jobs to people who had helped him get elected.

The lines grew longer whenever a new president came into office. After President Lincoln died, for instance, Andrew Johnson complained that the lines of job-seekers stretched down the stairs and out of the White House onto the lawn.

When James Garfield became president almost sixteen years later in 1881, thousands of people followed him to Washington in hopes of getting a government job. They went directly to the White House, crowding its corridors and calling out to the president as he passed.

One of those job-seekers was a thin, bearded man named Charles Julius Guiteau.

At the age of thirty-nine, Charles Guiteau was still searching for his place in life. Originally from Chicago, he had tried being a lawyer, a writer, a lecturer, a theologian, and a bill collector. None of these jobs ever seemed to work out, so he was always running out of money and piling up debts. And he had a terrible temper. He beat his wife and treated her so badly that the judge at their divorce hearing ordered Guiteau never to marry again.

In the summer of 1880, Guiteau's passions turned to interna-

■ Charles Guiteau

tional politics. He decided he wanted to be an ambassador to one of the great courts of Europe—the Austro–Hungarian empire.

Guiteau knew what he had to do in order to get the post. He had to work in the political campaign of someone who was running for president of the United States. If that candidate won, Guiteau would be rewarded with an important job.

So Guiteau picked a candidate: Ulysses S. Grant, the Union general who had served two terms as president after Andrew Johnson left office. Guiteau wrote a speech about former President Grant and was disappointed when the Republicans gave the nomination to someone else—an Ohio senator named James Garfield.

Guiteau got over his disappointment quickly. He reworked his campaign speech, changing every mention of former President Grant to Senator Garfield. (Fortunately, the two had a lot in common: Both were from Ohio, and both had been generals in the Civil War.) Guiteau delivered the speech at a campaign rally in New York, then sat back to await the election results.

When James Garfield won, Guiteau was elated. He packed his bags and headed for Washington. Arriving two days after the new president's inauguration, Guiteau went to the White House and found its corridors filled with other office seekers, all clutching speeches or letters or some other proof that they deserved the jobs they sought.

Guiteau knew he would have to do something special to stand out, so he pushed his way into a room where President Garfield was meeting with other men. Guiteau was ushered out of the room before he could speak to the president, but he was not discouraged.

He kept returning to the White House, always hoping for another chance to see the president. He left polite notes, offering President Garfield his advice and services. (When someone else was named ambassador to the Austro–Hungarian empire, Guiteau graciously offered to accept the position of counsel general in Paris.)

Weeks passed, and the president never responded to Guiteau's messages. After a couple of months, the White House ushers were told that Guiteau "should be quietly kept away." A secretary suggested that Guiteau try his luck at the State Department.

Guiteau managed to speak to Secretary of State James Blaine a few times, but eventually he was sent away from the State Department as well.

Meanwhile he was reading newspaper stories about a disagreement between the president and Senator Roscoe Conkling of New York, who was a leader of a group of Republicans known as Stalwarts. Conkling wanted President Garfield to put him in charge of handing out jobs to the Stalwarts in New York. But the president insisted on picking his own officeholders.

At first Guiteau sided with the president and wrote letters, telling him so. But then Guiteau began to wonder. He saw so many disappointed and angry office seekers in Washington that he imagined another civil war might start. This time, he thought, the war would be over government jobs and the way they were handed out.

One night Guiteau came up with a way to save the country.

"I was thinking over the political situation," he later wrote, "and the idea flashed through my brain that, if the president was out of the way, everything would go better."

At first the idea of killing the president horrified Guiteau. But he prayed until he decided that God approved. In fact, Guiteau became convinced that God had planted the idea in his head.

Like Booth, Guiteau thought killing the president would make him a hero. He thought he would be rewarded with an important government position when Vice President Chester Arthur became president.

In early June, Guiteau bought a revolver and a box of cartridges.

Of course, Guiteau realized that some people might not understand his decision to shoot the president. They might even put him in jail for a while, before Chester Arthur could rescue him. So Guiteau visited the District of Columbia jail to check out its facilities. He approved of what he saw, calling it "the best jail in America."

He also set about revising a religious book he had written several years earlier—*The Truth, a Companion to the Bible*. He figured thousands of people would want to buy the book and learn more about him after he saved the country from another civil war.

With his preparations complete, Guiteau began stalking the president. He followed President Garfield to a church service, to the train station, and to the secretary of state's house. Guiteau carried his revolver on these trips, but he never fired a shot. He came very close one time, but the sight of Mrs. Garfield—still thin and weak after a bout of malaria—stopped him.

When the summer heat began to settle over Washington, Mrs. Garfield took the family's three youngest children to a beach house in New Jersey. The two oldest sons, Hal and Jimmy, stayed in Washington with their father.

With Mrs. Garfield out of town, Guiteau began to follow the president's moves even more closely. He watched for the perfect moment to strike.

Then he read in the newspapers that the president and his sons intended to join the rest of the family for a Fourth of July celebration at the beach. From there, the Garfields planned to travel together through New England to the president's college reunion. They might even go back to their home in Ohio for a visit.

Guiteau saw he would have to act quickly. If he didn't kill the president now, he might not have another chance until fall.

The newspapers said the president was scheduled to leave Washington on a nine-thirty train on Saturday, July 2. Guiteau intended to be there.

On the night of July 1, 1881, Guiteau sat in his boardinghouse and wrote a letter explaining what he was about to do. He woke early the next morning and walked down to the river to take some practice shots with his gun. Then he went to the Baltimore and Potomac Depot at Sixth and B Streets, where he waited for the president.

President Garfield also woke early on the morning of July 2. He had been in office only four months, but he was already eager to leave the heat and worries of Washington behind.

His biggest worry had been about all of the people who wanted government jobs. He had tried to hand out the jobs fairly, but there just weren't enough positions for everyone. One newspaper estimated that twenty candidates applied for every job available. That meant whenever the president made an appointment, one person would be happy and nineteen would be disappointed.

Everywhere the president turned, he saw disappointed—and angry—office seekers. Even his argument with Senator Conkling and Vice President Arthur had been over government jobs. One night President Garfield wrote in his journal: "Some Civil Service Reform will come by necessity after the wearisome years of wasted Presidents have paved the way for it."

But the president wasn't feeling wearisome this morning. He joked with Hal and Jimmy, and talked about what they would do at the beach. He had invited six cabinet members—including Abraham Lincoln's son, Robert, who was now thirty-seven years old and secretary of war—to come along.

Secretary of State Blaine stopped at the White House around nine o'clock to give the president a ride to the train station. The boys went in another carriage.

President Garfield and Blaine arrived at the station early, so they sat in the carriage and talked for a few minutes. At nine-twenty they got out and entered the B Street door of the station.

They were walking through the ladies' waiting room, on their way to the general passenger area, when two pistol shots rang out behind them. The first bullet grazed the president's coat sleeve, and the second entered his back.

The president threw up his hands and cried, "My God, what is that?" Then he fell to the floor.

Blaine turned, saw Guiteau, and went after him. But a police officer tackled Guiteau first.

"I did it and will go to jail for it," Guiteau said. "Arthur is president, and I am a Stalwart."

Another officer arrived, and they hustled Guiteau to the police headquarters two blocks away. They didn't even stop to look for a gun.

Once they were at the station, the police found the revolver, still in Guiteau's pocket. They also found two letters Guiteau had written. One instructed the army to seize control of the jail where he expected to be taken. The other letter, addressed to the White House, said, "The President's tragic death was a sad necessity, but it will unite the Republican Party and save the Republic."

Inside the train station, blood spurted from a jagged wound near the president's spinal column. He vomited. A ladies' room attendant dropped to the floor and cradled the president's head in her lap, trying to comfort him.

■ Guiteau's attack on President Garfield

President Garfield's sons and cabinet members rushed to his side. Everyone saw the wound was serious. An army colonel told a reporter later that day, "I had seen too many men die on the battlefield not to know death's mark."

Dr. Smith Townsend, a District health officer who happened to be in the station at the time, stuck his finger in the wound. He was sure the injury was fatal, but he didn't want to frighten the president. So he told him the injury didn't look too serious.

"I thank you, Doctor," the president gasped, "but I am a dead man."

Someone brought a mattress from a sleeping car, and several men gently carried the president up a winding staircase to an empty railroad office on the second floor.

More doctors arrived and probed for the bullet. They could only shake their heads.

The president dictated a telegram to his wife, asking her to come. Then he told the men, "I think you had better get me to the White House as soon as you can."

They carried him back down the stairs to a horse-drawn ambulance, which rushed him to the White House. An excited crowd followed and waited anxiously outside its gates. Many people spoke in whispers of the terrifying night sixteen years before, when Abraham Lincoln had been shot.

Once again Robert Lincoln waited to see what would happen. "My God," he said, "how many hours of sorrow I have passed in this town."

The early news was not encouraging. Doctors still couldn't find the bullet, but they thought it had pierced the president's liver. "There is no hope for him," Dr. Willard Bliss told waiting reporters. "He will not probably live three hours, and may die in half an hour."

The next day's *New York Times* recorded the following exchange between the president and Dr. Bliss:

. . . the President asked Dr. Bliss what the prospects were. He said: "Are they bad, Doctor? Don't be afraid; tell me frankly. I am ready for the worst."

"Mr. President," replied Dr. Bliss, "your condition is extremely critical. I do not think you can live many hours."

"God's will be done, Doctor. I'm ready to go if my time has come," firmly responded the wounded man.

But his time hadn't come. At least not yet.

James Garfield survived that critical day. All across the nation, people prayed for him and took hope in small signs of recovery. Doctors issued regular bulletins that described his temperature, breathing, heartbeat, diet, and discomforts. When the president threw up, the whole country knew about it. When he asked for a sip of water in the middle of the night, everyone knew about that, too.

In the weeks that followed, doctors performed surgery on the president three times (once without anesthesia), but they never found the bullet. So they kept the wound open and issued regular, detailed reports about the pus discharge. Sometimes small pieces of bone or clothing showed up, and this excited a great deal of interest.

Doctors' reports were published in newspapers and displayed in shop windows. It seemed that everyone wanted to contribute to the president's comfort and recovery. On the day after the shooting, a Baltimore man sent a cow to the White House so the president could have fresh milk. Civil War veterans came to the White House so doctors could examine their bullet wounds—and perhaps learn something that would be useful in the president's case.

The doctors did not have X rays to help them locate the bullet. Alexander Graham Bell, who had invented the telephone five years before, came to the White House several times with an "electric probe," which he hoped would locate the bullet. But it didn't. (Doctors did not find the bullet until after the president's death. Then an autopsy showed that the bullet had taken a different path from what they had supposed; it had lodged in the president's pancreas.)

Without the antibiotics available today, President Garfield was subject to infections and terrible fevers. This, in the midst of Washington's sweltering summer, made him very uncomfortable. At first, the doctors covered his blankets with ice. Later, workmen rigged up a steam blower, which pushed air through a large "ice box" and into the president's bedroom. Some people worried that this early form of air conditioning was unhealthy, but President Garfield (and his doctors) seemed to enjoy the relief.

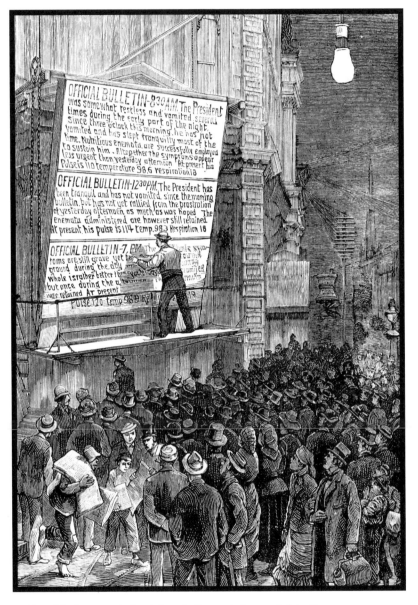

■ New Yorkers watched for daily updates outside the *New York Herald* offices. Smaller bulletins were posted in shop windows all over the country.

For a time, the doctors thought that the president might recover. A national day of thanksgiving was planned for the fall. But it was obvious that the president would not be able to perform his official duties for several months. The Constitution was clear about what happened when a president died: His vice president assumed the duties of the office. But what if a living president was unable to carry out his duties?

The Constitution didn't say, but several members of the president's cabinet thought Vice President Arthur should take over until the president was well again. Other cabinet members disagreed. Arthur, perhaps worried that he would appear too eager, made no move toward assuming power.

During the long weeks of his illness, President Garfield met with individual cabinet members briefly on a few occasions. He worried that he wasn't performing his duties as president. No one wanted him to strain himself, but he told his doctors that he was perfectly capable of signing his name. So they gave him an extradition paper that would return a prisoner to Canada, and he signed his name. That was his only official act in the sickroom.

As he began to feel better, he became anxious to leave the White House. He wanted to return to his home in Ohio, but that journey seemed too far. His doctors, concerned about the growing threat of malaria in Washington, decided he should go to the New Jersey cottage where Mrs. Garfield had been staying when he was shot. If all went well there, he could consider going on to Ohio.

The trip to New Jersey was planned carefully. Workers out-

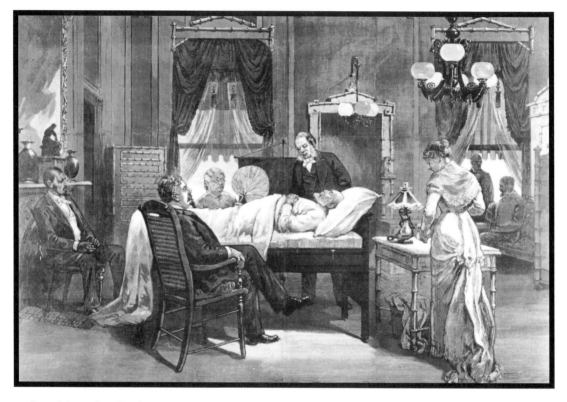

■ President Garfield endured the summer of 1881 in the White House.

fitted a special railroad car—complete with a water bed for the president's comfort—and covered the entire car with wire gauze. The night before the trip, three hundred men worked through the night to lay more than a half mile of additional track so the president's train could deliver him right to the front door of his cottage.

On the day of the trip, people stood quietly in the streets of Washington—and all along the two hundred miles of track—to show respect and concern for their president. The train never stopped, but the president's private secretary wrote bulletins and tossed them out the window to reporters waiting at train stations along the way.

After seven hours, the train arrived at Long Branch, New Jersey. At first the ocean breezes and fresh scenery seemed to do the president good. He even sat up in a chair for the first time since the shooting. Then the fever and vomiting returned.

On the evening of September 19, 1881—eighty days after the shooting—James Garfield cried out in pain. A few minutes later, he died.

Newspapers noted that this death seemed even crueler than Abraham Lincoln's. President Lincoln had died suddenly, at the end of a bloody war. But President Garfield's death came when the country was at peace. And people had followed his illness so long and so carefully that they felt they knew him like a member of their own family. They shared his mother's anguish when she cried, "If he had to die, why didn't God take him without all the terrible suffering he endured?"

The president's body lay in state in the rotunda of the Capitol in Washington for two days. Then thousands of people stood in silence along the railroad track and threw fresh flowers before the train that carried him back to Ohio.

Everyone had watched Garfield's sickroom all summer. Now they turned, in grief and anger, to Guiteau's jail cell.

Guiteau had been in solitary confinement ever since the shooting. During the president's long illness, he stayed in jail but was not charged with a crime. Authorities wanted to see what would happen to the president before they charged him with anything. Guiteau did not object to being held without charges; he saw quickly that Chester Arthur wasn't going to rescue him, and many others wanted to hang him. Jail was probably the safest place for him to be.

Even jail wasn't too safe. One of his guards shot at him but missed. Other guards reportedly had plans to torture and hang him.

Guiteau had not expected this reaction. He had thought he would be given great power and respect. (When a police officer whisked him past an angry mob right after the shooting, Guiteau promised to reward him by making him chief of police.)

But the expected power and glory never came. Guiteau began to worry about his trial.

He knew he would need money for lawyers and witnesses. He sent a letter to the White House, asking for a contribution. Chester Arthur owed him the money, Guiteau explained, because the shooting had raised his salary from $8,000 a year as vice president to $50,000 a year as president.

The new president did not reply to Guiteau's request.

Guiteau called on his training as a lawyer to come up with three defenses: First, President Garfield had died in New Jersey, and Guiteau had committed no crime in that state. Second, the shooting had not been fatal because the president lived so long afterward. (Guiteau blamed the president's death on incompetent medical care.) Third, Guiteau was not responsibile for the shooting because God had made him do it.

Guiteau's brother-in-law, George Scoville, acted as his lawyer. Scoville did not want the job—he had no experience in criminal trials—but no one else would take the case. (Eventually, two other attorneys joined Scoville, but he remained in charge and did most of the talking in court.)

Scoville dropped the New Jersey argument quickly. He blamed the doctors somewhat, but his major defense was that Guiteau was not guilty because he was insane.

Many people agreed that Guiteau must be insane. (Before he died, President Garfield himself had expressed that opinion.) At his trial, Guiteau certainly did not act like a normal man. He mumbled to himself and mocked the judge. He argued with witnesses and sometimes with his own attorneys. He insisted that he was not insane, but that his free will had been destroyed by God.

The trial lasted seventy-one days. On January 25, 1882, the jury took less than an hour to find Guiteau guilty of murdering the president of the United States.

He was hanged on June 30, 1882.

A few months later, Guiteau's sister, Frances Scoville, whose husband had defended Guiteau, was declared insane and committed to an asylum. Many people saw her illness as further proof that Guiteau had suffered from a hereditary mental illness.

Before she died, Mrs. Scoville wrote a novel about a man who was part of a conspiracy to kill the president of the United States.

Readers naturally saw the connection between her book and her brother, and rumors continued for many years about a possible conspiracy behind the death of James Garfield.

But most people saw his murder as the act of just one disappointed office seeker. Outraged that something like this could happen, both President Arthur and Congress started to dismantle the spoils system. In 1883, Congress passed the Pendleton Act to set up the Civil Service Commission, the agency that supervises the hiring of most government workers today.

The Civil Service Commission does not cover all government jobs. The president still appoints many officeholders, such as judges and ambassadors, who are not classified as part of the Civil Service. But the Civil Service Commission takes most government jobs out of the hands of politicians. As a result, getting and keeping a government job now depend more on *what* someone knows than *whom* someone knows.

Long lines still spill out of the White House, but the people today are waiting for tours, not jobs. The tours take visitors through the "public rooms" of the White House, not the rooms where the president and his family live and work. To visit those rooms, a person needs a special security clearance and an appointment.

But keeping the White House safe isn't enough. The most dangerous attacks have always come when the president leaves his home on Pennsylvania Avenue.

William McKinley

"Assassination is too easy here."
WHITE HOUSE DOORMAN

JAMES GARFIELD was not the only leader killed in 1881. In March of that year, a hand grenade exploded at the feet of Czar Alexander II of Russia, killing him instantly.

The Russian police quickly learned that the attacker—who also died in the explosion—had been an anarchist, someone opposed to government authority. Anarchists see no need for governments and work to overthrow those that exist. Some, obviously, were even willing to murder and die for the cause.

Over the next twenty years, anarchists killed several European leaders. Both the president of France and the empress of Austria were stabbed to death. The king of Italy died after an anarchist shot him.

But Europe was a long way from America, and no one thought anarchy was a problem here—until the summer of 1898, when someone investigating the Italian king's death came across a note naming six world leaders whom anarchists planned to kill. The note was at least two years old, and the first three people on the list were already dead. The fourth had survived several attacks. The fifth person on the list was William McKinley, president of the United States.

The note was passed along to President McKinley's advisers, who were naturally worried—and puzzled. Why would anarchists want to kill William McKinley? He hadn't been born into power like the kings and queens of Europe; he had been elected by his own people.

McKinley—or "Mac," as newspaper cartoonists liked to call him—was a popular president. Americans retold stories of his heroism as a young officer in the Civil War, and they were pleased with the way he had led the country's fight to liberate Cuba in the Spanish–American War. Now the economy was booming, and new inventions were being introduced almost every week.

It was easy to like Mac on a personal level, too. People admired his tender devotion to his sick wife. Ida Saxton had been a healthy young woman when she married William McKinley, but difficult childbirths and the deaths of their only children, two little girls,

■ Ida and William McKinley

had left her weak with epilepsy. She often suffered long and dangerous seizures.

In those days before the development of antiseizure drugs, people with epilepsy were often hidden away. Some people whispered about the "scenes" Mrs. McKinley made in public, but her husband proudly took her everywhere. He changed the seating arrangements at state dinners so he could sit next to her, ready to drop a handkerchief over her face if a seizure contorted her features.

But no matter how much people liked and admired the president, his advisers—who had lived through the assassinations of Abraham Lincoln and James Garfield—knew personal popularity couldn't protect him from a determined assassin. So they looked for someone to guard the president.

Until now, the protection of presidents had been casual at best. A few ceremonial guards stood at the White House; and sometimes District of Columbia police officers, soldiers, or Secret Service agents accompanied the president when he left the White House. But the president usually rode and walked around Washington alone.

After seeing the anarchists' note, President McKinley's advisers asked the Secret Service to assign someone to guard the president at all times. In some ways, the Secret Service was an odd choice; it had started as a spy agency during the Civil War, assigned to detect counterfeit money and stamps. Looking for "funny money" was a long way from guarding the president, but Secret Service agents occasionally did other kinds of police work as well. So agent George Foster was assigned to protect the president.

From the beginning, President McKinley did not like the idea of having a personal guard. He often slipped away from Foster for a stroll or a carriage ride with his wife. And he insisted on being treated as a private—and unguarded—citizen on his visits to his home in Canton, Ohio.

But Foster took his job seriously. People in Washington often saw him trotting on foot alongside the president's carriage, with his sharp eyes watching for danger.

. . .

Meanwhile, on an Ohio farm, the son of a Polish immigrant was reading about the assassinations in Europe. Twenty-eight-year-old Leon Czolgosz was so fascinated that he took old newspapers to bed with him every night so he could reread the stories.

Czolgosz admired the anarchists who committed these crimes. He thought rulers were the enemies of working people. And the enemies, he thought, should be killed.

But some of the stories from Europe angered Czolgosz. He read about several anarchists who shot at their targets but missed. Czolgosz was sure they were trying to shoot from too far away, probably because they wanted to give themselves a better chance of escape.

A true anarchist, Czolgosz thought, shouldn't worry about his own safety. He should shoot the ruler close up, then turn himself in to the police and accept his punishment as a martyr to the cause of anarchy.

In the spring of 1901, Czolgosz decided he had done enough reading about anarchists; he wanted to become one himself. He took his share of the money from the family farm and began making trips, first to Cleveland, then to Chicago, and then to Buffalo. He returned to Cleveland several times and once heard a lecture there by a famous anarchist named Emma Goldman. "Miss Goldman's words went right through me," Czolgosz later said, "and when I left the lecture, I had made up my mind that I would have to do something heroic for the cause I loved."

He tried to meet Emma Goldman and other leaders of the anarchy movement, but no one paid attention to him. He started calling himself Fred Niemann—Fred Nobody.

But Czolgosz wasn't going to be a Nobody for long.

He was in Chicago when he read in a newspaper that President McKinley planned to attend the Pan-American Exposition in Buffalo. The fair celebrated a century of progress, and the president was expected to give an important speech about his plans to change the way America traded its products with other countries.

Czolgosz put down his newspaper and bought a train ticket to Buffalo. When he arrived there, he found everyone excited about the president's visit. The leaders of the exposition had declared September 5, the day of McKinley's speech, "President's Day."

Czolgosz was disgusted. "All those people seemed [to be] bowing to the great ruler," he said later. "I made up my mind to kill that ruler. I bought a .32-caliber revolver and loaded it."

When the McKinleys arrived at the fairgrounds on the third of September, Czolgosz was waiting. But the police and the jostling crowds kept pushing him back, so he couldn't get close to the president.

"They forced everybody back, so the great ruler could pass," he later complained.

Czolgosz followed McKinley the next day and the day after that. He listened to the big speech, but he didn't cheer with everyone else. He just watched for his opportunity, a clear shot at the president.

Some people suggested later that Czolgosz hesitated to shoot because he was afraid of what the crowds or the police might do to him. But Czolgosz insisted he had no concern about his personal safety: "I was not afraid of them, or that I would get hurt, but afraid I might be seized and that my chance would be gone forever."

On the fourth day, he heard that the president planned to greet people at a public reception in the Temple of Music, a large ornate building on the fairgrounds.

Czolgosz went to the Temple of Music early, so he would be one of the first people in line to meet the president.

From the beginning, President McKinley's advisers had not liked the idea of a public reception. His secretary, George Cortelyou, had taken it off the president's schedule twice, but President McKinley insisted on putting it back. True politician that he was, William McKinley wanted to meet people and shake their hands.

When Cortelyou asked the president one last time to give up the reception, President McKinley said, "Why should I? No one would wish to hurt me."

Indeed, everyone at the fair seemed friendly—and eager to see the president and his wife. Mrs. McKinley, overwhelmed by the crowds pressing in on them, agreed the public reception would be too much for her to handle. She decided to spend the afternoon at the home of John Milburn, president of the exposition.

Still worried about the crowds, Cortelyou and Foster brought in extra soldiers to guard the aisle leading to the president at the Tem-

■ The McKinleys, going to the fair on the morning of September 6, 1901

ple of Music. Unfortunately, these extra soldiers also blocked Foster's view, so he couldn't get a good look at the people approaching the president.

The east doorway to the Temple of Music was opened at four o'clock on the afternoon of September 6, 1901. People came in two by two and formed a single file as the aisle narrowed. The president stood on a raised platform, shaking hands.

It was a hot day, and several people used handkerchiefs to wipe their brows. So it didn't seem unusual when Leon Czolgosz pulled a handkerchief out of his pocket.

Standing next to the president, Cortelyou noticed the handkerchief—and a bulge beneath it—but he assumed the man's hand had been injured and was in bandages. He was more worried about a suspicious-looking man just ahead of Czolgosz.

Foster had noticed this man, too, and was watching him carefully. He moved close to the man and walked beside him as he approached the president.

Cortelyou and Foster were both relieved when the fellow shook the president's hand and moved on. Next in line were a little girl and her mother. President McKinley shook the woman's hand and patted the child on the head. Then he turned with a smile to the next in line, Leon Czolgosz.

Czolgosz pushed the president's extended hand aside and fired two shots through the handkerchief covering his gun.

For a moment, silence fell on the Temple of Music. William McKinley stood still, just looking at Czolgosz.

Then Foster and two other men—including the one who had drawn such suspicion—pounced on Czolgosz and threw him to the floor.

The president took a step backward, then turned and walked steadily to a chair a few feet away. Cortelyou rushed to his side, and more people jumped on Czolgosz, threatening to hang him.

"Don't let them hurt him," McKinley said.

"But you are wounded!" Cortelyou cried. "Here, let me examine."

"No, I think not," the president said. "I am not badly hurt, I assure you."

Cortelyou loosened President McKinley's clothes and found a bloodstain spreading across his white linen shirt.

■ Czolgosz's attack on President McKinley

"My wife," the president whispered. "Be careful, Cortelyou, how you tell her—oh, be careful!"

Mrs. McKinley was napping when her husband was shot. When word reached the Milburn house of the shooting, everyone worried about whether they should awaken Mrs. McKinley. Afraid the news would shock her into a dangerous seizure, they decided to let her sleep.

Telephone communication was cut off to the home, and no one told Ida McKinley what had happened, even after she awoke and took up her afternoon crocheting. When darkness began to fall around seven o'clock that evening, she asked where her husband was.

Still, no one told her until her doctor arrived to break the news. He later told the newspapers that she "stood it bravely."

Within minutes of the shooting, a motor ambulance pulled up in front of the Temple of Music. The president was carried out on a stretcher and taken to the emergency hospital at the fairgrounds. The hospital was little more than a first-aid station, but the doctors decided to perform surgery immediately.

One bullet fell out as they removed the president's clothes. But another was deeply, dangerously inside his body.

The president said the Lord's Prayer as ether was administered.

When the doctors opened his abdomen, they found the second

bullet had torn through his stomach. They stitched the holes in his stomach together, but they could not find the bullet. (A new contraption called an X-ray machine was on display at the fairgrounds, but apparently no one thought of trying to use it.)

As the afternoon light faded, one of the doctors managed to rig up an electric light so the others could finish the surgery. Then the ambulance took the president to the Milburn home, where Mrs. McKinley waited.

The doctors were optimistic, but many Americans naturally remembered the long deathwatch for James Garfield twenty years before.

"I feel certain President McKinley will get well," one of the surgeons insisted. "This is not 1881, but 1901, and great strides have been made in surgery in the past twenty years."

Czolgosz offered no resistance to the police after the shooting. "I am an anarchist," he proclaimed. "I am a disciple of Emma Goldman. Her words set me on fire."

Those words set the country on fire.

Many Americans demanded that anarchists be forced to leave the country. Some hunted down anarchists and burned their homes.

The mayor of Cliffside, New Jersey, advised the widow of a well-known anarchist (the one who had shot the king of Italy) to leave town. The widow refused, saying she was not an anarchist.

"I suppose that I will be hounded in every place I go, and

■ Leon Czolgosz

branded as a anarchist," she told reporters. "People would like to see me driven to the poorhouse and left there to die."

Of course, the most despised anarchist was Emma Goldman herself. A nationwide search for her began. Four days after the shooting, she was arrested in Chicago, where she was using another name.

"I never advocated violence," she said. "I scarcely knew him [Czolgosz]."

Czolgosz insisted he had acted alone, but the police were sure he must have been part of a plot. They said anarchists had probably drawn lots to see who would kill the president.

Dozens more anarchists were arrested, but police could never find a connection between them and Czolgosz.

"We do not know him, but he is one of us," said a New Jersey anarchist. "He did what it was his duty to do, and we honor him while personally thinking his effort might better have been employed across the ocean upon some crowned head."

Hundreds of people gathered outside the Milburn house in Buffalo. Across the street, newspaper reporters set up tents, sheltering telegraph machines that ticked news of the president's condition across the country.

Vice President Theodore Roosevelt and members of the cabinet rushed to Buffalo. By the time they arrived, the president's condition had improved and doctors were saying he was "on the high road to recovery." They predicted he would be back to work within three or four weeks.

The nation rejoiced in the good news. Vice President Roosevelt was so confident that he left Buffalo for a hunting trip in the Adirondack Mountains, even though that put him twelve miles from the nearest telephone or telegraph.

Only Secretary of State John Hay was grim. He had been President Lincoln's secretary and President Garfield's close friend. He was convinced that this president would die, too.

Robert Lincoln, now fifty-eight years old, also visited the Milburn house, but he didn't tell reporters what he thought of the president's prospects.

The doctors continued to be optimistic. "Good news! Good news!" one doctor told reporters five days after the shooting. The president's wounds had healed, he said, with no signs of blood poisoning.

The president was certainly feeling better. Forbidden to see newspapers, he was eager to hear about the reaction to his speech. "How was it received abroad?" he asked.

But the doctors wanted him to rest. They allowed no visitors except his wife and Cortelyou. "It's mighty lonesome in here," the president complained.

On September 13, the doctors reported a "sinking spell." Antibiotics were still not available to fight infections, and gangrene was setting in along the bullet's path. Ever since the shooting, the president had been receiving liquid nourishment through a tube in his rectum, but now everything was being ejected.

No one understood this sudden turn for the worse. Newspapers carried speculations that the bullet had been poisoned or that the president had been weakened by a "tobacco heart," created by years of smoking cigars.

No matter what the cause, it was clear the president was dying. He awoke for a few moments and looked at the doctors gathered around his bed.

"It is useless, gentlemen," he said. "I think we ought to have a prayer."

He asked for his wife. He put his arm around her. "Good-bye— good-bye, all," he said. "It is God's way. His will, not ours, be done." Then he began to whisper the words of a favorite hymn, "Nearer, My God, to Thee."

William McKinley died at two-fifteen, on the morning of September 14.

For twelve hours the country had no president. The search for Vice President Roosevelt had begun during McKinley's sinking spell. A guide finally found him high on Mount Marcy in the Adirondacks.

When he heard the president was dying, Roosevelt scrambled down the mountain and rode three relays of horses over mountain roads to a special train, which carried him back to Buffalo. Once there, he took the presidential oath of office at the home of a friend.

An autopsy showed William McKinley died of gangrene. The second bullet was never recovered, even though doctors searched for almost four hours. "It is probably embedded in the fatty tissue of the back," one said. The doctors dismissed the idea that the bullet had been poisoned.

Once again the nation was in mourning, and state services were being planned. Newspapers speculated that Mrs. McKinley might not survive the strain of her grief.

She begged to sit with the rest of the president's family at services held at the Milburn home. But the family and her doctors worried about her seizures. So they made her sit at the top of the staircase, out of sight, where she could hear the prayers and hymns.

A special train returned the president's body to Washington, where a silent crowd waited in the streets. One woman's clear voice began singing "Nearer, My God, to Thee," and soon hundreds—maybe thousands—joined in.

William McKinley's body lay in state, just as the bodies of Abraham Lincoln and James Garfield had, in the East Room of the White House and the rotunda of the Capitol. On the day of the funeral, thousands of people stampeded to get inside the Capitol, and three hundred people were crushed. No one died, but the Capitol was turned into a hospital of sorts, with almost every room being used for emergency care.

The president's body was taken to Canton, where he was buried with his daughters. The doctors said Mrs. McKinley was too ill to attend the services.

Within an hour of the president's death, the warden at Auburn Prison in New York began receiving requests to witness the execution of Czolgosz. The trial seemed to be a mere formality.

No lawyer wanted to defend Czolgosz, but two retired judges reluctantly agreed to do so. The trial began in Buffalo on September 24, just ten days after the president's death; it lasted eight hours and twenty-six minutes.

The jury took thirty-five minutes to convict Czolgosz of first-degree murder.

He was strapped into an electric chair and executed on October 29. Carbolic acid was poured in Czolgosz's coffin so his body would disintegrate within twelve hours.

Ida McKinley left Washington and returned to Canton. The Roosevelt family moved into the White House, filling it with children, ponies, dogs, cats, birds, guinea pigs, lizards, a badger, a small bear, and a snake named Emily Spinach. At forty-two, Teddy Roosevelt was the youngest president in American history, and his family made the White House a lively place.

But the shadow of William McKinley's death lingered over the country. Before then, most Americans thought events in places like Russia and Europe were too far away to affect them. But now, in the twentieth century, they were beginning to see that problems across the ocean could quickly become problems at home.

Congress passed new laws aimed at protecting the president. The immigration laws were changed to forbid anarchists from entering the country. And the Secret Service was expanded so guarding the president and his family became its main job.

Today the Secret Service has hundreds of agents dedicated to protecting the president, the vice president, and their families. (Agents also guard candidates for national office and visiting leaders from other countries.)

Secret Service agents take an oath, promising to give up their own lives in order to protect the president's. When you see the president on TV, you can often see Secret Service agents nearby, ever watchful.

But no one can protect the president from all danger. An old White House doorman—who stayed with Tad Lincoln the night his father was shot and who later helped pack Ida McKinley's trunks—made this sad commentary:

"It looks as though we would have to keep the president in a fort and search all visitors before letting them in to talk to him. Assassination is too easy here."

Keeping the President Safe

"A president has to expect
these things."
HARRY S. TRUMAN

THE SECRET SERVICE, a private citizen, and good luck protected the next three presidents who faced gunmen.

Theodore Roosevelt was the lucky one. He served out the rest of William McKinley's term, then was elected president on his own. He left the White House in 1909 after his friend and Secretary of War, William Howard Taft, was elected president.

Colonel Roosevelt, as he liked to be called now, disagreed with President Taft about some issues and decided to run for president again in 1912. The Republicans, though, renominated President

Taft and the Democrats nominated a former college professor named Woodrow Wilson. So Colonel Roosevelt formed his own political party, called the Bull Moose Party.

■ Theodore Roosevelt campaigning

Colonel Roosevelt was on his way to a campaign rally in Milwaukee on October 14, 1912, when a man stepped out of a crowd and shot him in the chest.

The bullet tore through Colonel Roosevelt's coat, his spectacle case, and a folded copy of the speech he was about to give. It came to rest in his ribs. (If the speech hadn't been so thick, the bullet surely would have killed him.)

Some people in the crowd grabbed the man and threatened to hang him. But Colonel Roosevelt shouted, "Stand back! Don't hurt that man!"

With blood on his shirt and the bullet still in him, Colonel Roosevelt went ahead and gave his speech. He later went to a hospital and had the bullet removed. The other candidates announced they would stop campaigning while he recuperated.

Everyone admired Teddy Roosevelt's courage (and luck), but he did not win the election. With traditional Republican voters divided between Colonel Roosevelt and President Taft, Democrat Woodrow Wilson won the election and became the twenty-eighth president of the United States.

The gunman, identified as John F. Schrank of New York City, told police the ghost of William McKinley had told him to shoot his former vice president. Judged insane, Schrank spent the rest of his life in a mental hospital.

Theodore Roosevelt's distant cousin—Franklin Delano Roosevelt—was saved by a quick-thinking woman in early 1933. In those days, presidential elections were held in November, as they are today, but the inaugurations weren't held until the following March. So Franklin Roosevelt, elected in November 1932, wouldn't be sworn in until March 1933.

While he waited, the president-elect went on a fishing vacation with some friends off the Florida coast. On February 15, 1933, they visited Miami, where President-elect Roosevelt—whose legs had been paralyzed by polio several years earlier—sat in an open touring car, laughing and talking with people who had come to see him.

Suddenly a curly-haired young man jumped onto a bench, pointed a pistol at the president-elect, and began firing. A woman

■ Because Franklin Roosevelt could not walk without assistance, he often campaigned and talked with people from the passenger seat of a car.

standing next to the shooter—Lillian Cross of Miami—grabbed at the man's arm so the bullets went off in a different direction. They hit five other people—including Chicago mayor Anthony Cermak—but missed Franklin Roosevelt.

The crowd jumped on the gunman. "I'm all right! I'm all right!" Roosevelt assured everyone.

His driver started to take off, but Roosevelt saw Mayor Cermak doubled over. He told the driver to stop. The Secret Service agents—following the standard policy of immediately removing the president (or, in this case, the president-elect) from any dangerous situation—shouted at the driver to leave. Franklin Roosevelt again ordered him to wait. The driver waited while Mayor Cermak was placed in the car.

As the car finally began to move through the crowd, the president-elect cradled Mayor Cermak in his arms and tried to find his pulse. "Tony, keep quiet—don't move," he said. "It won't hurt you if you keep quiet."

Franklin Roosevelt waited at the hospital while his friend was rushed into surgery. After the operation, the mayor whispered to him, "I'm glad it was me instead of you."

The gunman—an unemployed bricklayer named Giuseppe Zangara—told police he was an anarchist. "I want to make it clear I do not hate Mr. Roosevelt personally," he said. "I hate all presidents, no matter from what country they come, and I hate all officials and everybody who is rich."

Within a week of the shooting, Zangara was tried, convicted, and sentenced to eighty years in prison. After Mayor Cermak died on March 6, Zangara was tried again—this time for murder. He was convicted and sentenced to death in the electric chair. He was executed on March 20, a little more than a month after the shooting.

Franklin Roosevelt remained president through the end of the Depression and through most of World War II. When he died in 1945, his vice president—Harry S. Truman—became president.

President Truman worried more about plaster falling on his head than about getting shot. That's because the old White House, neglected during the Depression and the war years, was falling apart. A piano broke through a sitting-room floor, and chandeliers swayed dangerously over guests at state dinners.

When engineers inspected the White House in 1948, they found it in danger of collapsing at any moment. The Trumans moved across the street to Blair House, where foreign guests often stayed, so repairs could begin.

The repairs took more than three years to complete, and the Secret Service was naturally nervous about having the president stay in Blair House so long. It was much smaller and closer to the street than the White House. On hot days, only a screen door separated the president from people on the sidewalk.

November 1, 1950, was one of those hot days. With the temperature in the eighties (and still no air-conditioning available), the president stripped to his underwear and stretched out on his bed upstairs with the windows open.

Suddenly he heard gunfire on the street below. Two men—apparently seeking the independence of Puerto Rico—were running toward Blair House from opposite directions and shooting. They planned to shoot their way into the house and kill the president.

The men—Griselio Torresola and Oscar Collazo—fired their guns at the three guards stationed outside Blair House. One of the guards was shot in the leg, but managed to drag himself to the street and pull the gunfire away from the house.

In the blaze of gunfire, Collazo rushed up the front steps. He was reaching for the screen door when two guards shot him down. He tried to get up but was shot again.

Torresola shot another guard, Leslie Coffelt, in the chest and abdomen. Coffelt was bleeding to death when he pulled off one last shot, which killed Torresola.

After three minutes (and twenty-seven shots), the gunfire stopped. A guard and a would-be assassin were dead; two guards and the other would-be assassin were seriously injured.

Mrs. Truman looked out an upstairs window. "Harry," she called, "someone's shooting our policemen!"

The president rushed to the window, but Secret Service agents yelled at him. "Get back!" they cried. "Get back!"

He got back.

Then he dressed and went downstairs to see what was going on. The Secret Service agents again told him to stay back. A few minutes later, he slipped out the back door to keep an appointment to dedicate a statue at Arlington Cemetery, across the river, in Virginia.

Meanwhile rumors swept through Washington. Some people said the president had been killed, along with seven Secret Service agents. But Harry Truman remained calm. "A president has to expect these things," he said.

Collazo was later sentenced to death, but President Truman changed his sentence to life imprisonment. He said he did not be-

■ The body of Griselio Torresola, after the attack on President Truman

lieve in capital punishment, even for someone who had tried to kill him.

The Secret Service mourned the death of Leslie Coffelt, but it was proud. No president had been killed since Congress had given the Secret Service the job of protecting the president in 1901.

That record would be broken on November 22, 1963.

"The president is dead."
CBS ANCHORMAN WALTER CRONKITE

OVER THE YEARS Americans began to notice a strange pattern: Every twenty years the country had elected a president who later died in office.

Of course, not every president was assassinated; some died of natural causes. William Henry Harrison, the first victim of what came to be known as the Twenty-Year Curse, was elected in 1840 and died of pneumonia only six weeks after his inauguration. Then Abraham Lincoln (elected in 1860), James Garfield (elected in 1880), and William McKinley (reelected in 1900) were shot.

The curse continued when Warren G. Harding (elected in 1920) and Franklin Delano Roosevelt (reelected in 1940) died.* The exact cause of President Harding's death is still a mystery—maybe it was food poisoning, maybe it was pneumonia, or maybe it was something else. The cause of President Roosevelt's death, though, was clear; he had a cerebral hemorrhage, which means a blood vessel in his brain burst.

When John Fitzgerald Kennedy was elected president in 1960, a reporter reminded him of the Twenty-Year Curse. "Well, that's one tradition that we'll have to break," Kennedy said.

Nineteen sixty looked like a good year to end the tragic tradition. Secret Service agents were now legendary for the careful way they protected the president. And Jack Kennedy was so young and energetic. He was forty-three years old when he was elected president. Like Theodore Roosevelt, he brought a young family to the White House. He and his wife, Jacqueline, had a three-year-old daughter, Caroline, and a baby son, John Fitzgerald Kennedy, Jr., born just three weeks after his father's election.

The newspapers were fascinated with the president's young family. Later, some said the Kennedys, with their grace and style, transformed the White House into Camelot, the legendary land where King Arthur had lived with his Knights of the Round Table.

But many people hated President Kennedy. Some of the hatred

* Only one president died outside the Twenty-Year Curse: Zachary Taylor, who had been elected in 1848, died of typhoid fever in 1850.

85

came from people who didn't like Catholics. Jack Kennedy was the country's first Catholic president, and some people honestly believed he would let the Pope run the country. (Of course, he didn't.)

Even more hatred came from people who opposed the civil rights movement. One hundred years after the Civil War, many states still had laws that kept African-American people from voting, getting good jobs, living in white neighborhoods, entering restaurants, using public drinking fountains, and sending their children to schools with white children. President Kennedy opposed segregation, and he expressed outrage when people who stood up for their rights were killed.

President Kennedy also opposed Communism. A World War II hero, he believed the Communist leaders in the Soviet Union were serious when they promised to take over the world. The president sent "military advisers" to tiny countries all over the world—including Vietnam—to fight the spread of Communism.

He was especially concerned with Cuba, just ninety miles off the Florida coast, where Communist Fidel Castro had come into power. Early in his presidency, John Kennedy planned a secret invasion of Cuba, which failed. He later demanded that the Soviet Union remove missiles in Cuba that were aimed at the United States. When the Soviets refused, the president went on national television to warn Americans that a nuclear war might begin.

But the big bomb never fell. The Soviets removed their missiles, and the newspapers said President Kennedy had won this show-down with the Communists.

While President Kennedy was fighting Communism, a former Marine named Lee Harvey Oswald was embracing it. Oswald's life certainly didn't resemble anything in Camelot. He was poor, not well educated, and resentful of the good life he was missing.

After his discharge from the Marines, Oswald went to the Soviet Union, with the idea of becoming a Soviet citizen and an active member of the Communist Party. He thought he might even become a spy. Soviet officials talked with him but decided they didn't want him as a spy. They didn't even want him to stay in their country. They ordered Oswald to leave the Soviet Union at once.

Oswald was so upset that he tried to kill himself by slashing his wrists. An ambulance rushed him to a hospital, where blood trans-fusions saved his life.

The officials worried they would be blamed if this American succeeded in killing himself. They decided to let him stay in the Soviet Union without becoming a citizen.

Oswald married a Russian woman, Marina Prusakova, but grew tired of life in a country where he wasn't wanted. He brought his wife back to Texas, where their daughter was born.

The Oswalds' new life in the United States was hard. Oswald had trouble keeping a job and began beating his wife. He wanted to

■ Maria Oswald took this photograph of her husband, Lee Harvey Oswald, in their backyard.

do something important with his life—something people would notice. He bought a rifle through a mail-order catalog and shot at a former army general who had spoken at several anti-Communist rallies. He missed and was disappointed when newspapers didn't even report the attack.

Although he was still fascinated by Communism, Oswald could not forgive the Soviet Union for the way it had rejected him. He decided he preferred the way Communism was practiced in Cuba. Outraged by President Kennedy's invasion of Cuba, he started a Fair Play for Cuba Committee. He handed out pamphlets urging "Hands Off Cuba!" on street corners in New Orleans, where he had gone to look for work. When he still couldn't find a job, he decided to go to Cuba.

The United States had forbidden travel to Cuba, so Oswald took a bus to Mexico City, hoping to reach his destination from there. But no one at the Cuban or the Soviet embassies would help him. Disappointed, he returned to his wife and daughter in Irving, Texas, where he began plotting more ways to help the Communist cause.

He told his wife he was going to shoot Richard Nixon, who was then a former vice president with a reputation for fighting Communism. Then he said he was going to hijack an airplane to Cuba. Leaping around the apartment in his underwear, he practiced what he would do on the plane.

"Junie," Marina Oswald whispered to their daughter, "our papa is out of his mind."

While Oswald planned his next escapade, his wife was expecting another baby and the family still needed to eat. His wife had made a friend who helped him find a new job, this time at the Texas

School Book Depository in Dallas. During the week he stayed at a boardinghouse in Dallas; on weekends he went back to Irving, where his family was staying with the friend.

Oswald had been working at the depository for almost a month when he read a day-old newspaper that said President Kennedy was coming to Dallas on November 22. A map showed the president's motorcade would go right by the Texas School Book Depository.

President Kennedy—who had done so much to fight Communism in Cuba—was a much more important target than a retired army general or a former vice president. Oswald began to see his place in history.

He went back to Irving on Thursday, November 21. His wife was surprised to see him because it was the middle of the week. She was even more surprised the next morning when she saw he had left his wedding ring and $170—almost all of their savings—on the dresser in their bedroom.

What she didn't know was that he had taken his rifle back to Dallas.

He apparently hid it in a large paper bag fashioned out of wrapping paper he'd taken from the depository. When a co-worker gave him a ride the next morning, Oswald told him the package contained curtain rods.

Several people warned President Kennedy not to go to Dallas. They'd seen or heard about posters and newspaper ads in Dallas that accused Kennedy of treason; one even showed him with a bull's-eye on his forehead. The city was too dangerous, they said.

But the president said he had to go. Two Texas Democrats— Governor John Connally and Senator Ralph Yarborough—were arguing, and Kennedy wanted to settle their feud before the 1964 presidential election.

The president also had a personal reason for looking forward to the Dallas trip. Three months before, the Kennedys had had another baby, but little Patrick had died when he was only two days old. Heartbroken, Mrs. Kennedy had avoided public appearances, but now she was willing to go to Dallas with her husband. This would be the Kennedys' first trip together since the baby's death.

On Thursday, November 21, 1963, the Kennedys left Washington and flew to San Antonio, Texas. From there they flew to Houston and then to Fort Worth. At every airport hundreds of people reached out to shake the Kennedys' hands, and thousands of people lined the streets to cheer them.

Occasionally the Kennedys saw a negative poster or heard someone shout insults, but mostly they saw friendly faces, delighted to see their young president and his pretty wife.

They spent the night in Fort Worth, then got up early on the morning of November 22 for a ten-minute flight to Dallas. When their plane landed at Love Field, Mrs. Kennedy was given a bouquet of yellow roses, the state flower of Texas.

■ President Kennedy and his wife, Jacqueline, arriving at Love Field in Dallas

The Kennedys got into the presidential limousine with Governor Connally and his wife, Nelly, to begin a motorcade through downtown Dallas. The car—a long blue convertible—had a protective bubble top, but it was removed because President Kennedy wanted to make sure the crowds could see him clearly.

Another sharp sound, and President Kennedy grabbed at his throat. He slumped just a little, but he didn't duck or fall over. (Back problems caused the president to wear a metal brace, which kept him erect.)

Governor Connally fell forward, also hit. "No, no, no, no, no!" he yelled. "They're going to kill us both!"

Mrs. Kennedy reached out for her husband. Another shot hit his head. Blood and brain tissue spurted everywhere, and the president fell into her lap. "My God, I've got his brains in my hand!" Mrs. Kennedy cried.

At last the driver pressed his foot to the accelerator. As the car picked up speed, Mrs. Kennedy crawled over the backseat and onto the trunk. Some people think she was reaching for part of the president's skull that had blown off, and some people think she was trying to get away. Others think she was trying to help a Secret Service agent who had caught hold of the speeding car. (Mrs. Kennedy later said she didn't remember what she was trying to do.)

Somehow the Secret Service agent got onto the car and pushed Mrs. Kennedy back inside. They sped toward Parkland Hospital.

The president still had a faint pulse, and the emergency room doctors worked to save him. They cut a hole in his throat (over one of the bullet wounds) and inserted a tube to make breathing easier. And they massaged his chest, trying to get his heart pumping.

They talked about opening his chest to massage his heart directly. But one of the doctors looked at the president's head wound and realized about one third of his brain had been blown away. "I think you better look at this first," he told the other doctors. "We have no way of resuscitating him. I think it's time to declare him dead."

Two priests (who had heard of the shooting and hurried to the hospital) administered the last sacrament of the Catholic Church.

At one o'clock the doctors declared President Kennedy dead.

The entire country was stunned. Schools and stores closed. People stopped each other on the street to share the terrible news. Many went to church, but most turned to their television sets. CBS anchorman Walter Cronkite wept as he reported the news of the president's death.

For the next three days, the TV networks provided continuous coverage of the tragedy; they didn't even play commercials. People stayed by their TV sets, watching and listening to events as they unfolded.

They heard Governor Connally had been rushed into surgery and Vice President Johnson had been led through winding corridors to a small room where the shades were drawn. They understood the Secret Service had been afraid someone would attack him, too.

At Dealey Plaza, confused people cried and ran in all directions. The buildings surrounding the green, open space had created an echo chamber, so the sounds of gunfire had bounced around. Many witnesses weren't sure how many shots had been fired. Some said they had heard just two shots, but others said they'd heard three, four, or more separate shots.

People were also confused about where the shots had come from. Most thought the shots had come from the Texas School Book Depository building. (A home movie, photographed by Abraham Zapruder on Dealey Plaza, shows the Kennedys and the Connallys all turned to look back at the depository building after the first shot.) But others thought at least one shot had come from a grassy knoll across the street from the building.

A Dallas policeman entered the depository building and began a floor-by-floor search. He found Oswald in the second-floor lunchroom, drinking a Coke, fifteen minutes after the shooting.

The building manager, accompanying the policeman, identified Oswald as someone who worked at the depository. They let him go and continued their search.

On the sixth floor, they found a sniper's nest—the rifle and three empty cartridge cases hidden by a stack of cartons near an open window. They found a palmprint on the rifle barrel that turned out to be Oswald's.

Meanwhile, Oswald walked out the front door of the building. A television reporter stopped him to ask where the nearest telephone was, and Oswald pointed it out. Then he continued walking until he caught a bus seven blocks away.

When the bus became trapped in traffic, he got off, ran three blocks, and caught a cab, which dropped him off a few blocks from his boardinghouse. He ran into his room, grabbed a pistol and a jacket, and left.

About ten minutes later, a Dallas policeman named J. D. Tippit stopped Oswald beside a drugstore. Oswald apparently shot him four times, killing him. Then he darted through a gas station, across a parking lot, and down eight blocks to a movie theatre. He ducked inside the theatre without buying a ticket.

By now, everyone in Dallas was looking for the man who had shot the president. The movie ticket-taker—who had heard a description of the shooter—called the police.

The police went into the darkened theatre, flipped on the lights, and spotted Oswald. When he saw the police, Oswald shouted, "Well, it's all over now!"

He pulled out his pistol and tried to shoot again, but the police overpowered him. As they took him out of the theatre, he shouted, "I protest this police brutality!"

When they heard President Kennedy was dead, Lyndon Johnson and his aides decided to return to Washington at once. Johnson crouched on the floor of a car as it sped toward the airport. Secret Service agents hurried him onto Air Force One, the presidential airplane, and told the pilot to take off.

But Johnson insisted they wait for Mrs. Kennedy. And Mrs. Kennedy refused to leave the hospital without her husband's body. One of President Kennedy's aides called a funeral director, who brought a red bronze coffin to the hospital.

Just as Mrs. Kennedy was preparing to leave with the body, the chief medical examiner of Dallas County stepped forward. A murder had been committed in Dallas, he said, and the law required an autopsy before the body could be moved outside the county.

President Kennedy's aides argued with him, but the medical examiner was stubborn. (There was still no federal law prohibiting presidential assassinations, so he said the case had to follow the local rules of investigation.)

Angry and anxious to leave Dallas, the aides pushed the coffin past him, loaded it on an ambulance, and sped to the airport.

Even after Mrs. Kennedy and the coffin were aboard, Air Force One did not take off. Lyndon Johnson wanted to take the oath of office on the ground. One of his old friends, Judge Sarah T. Hughes, hurried (as much as she could, in the snarled traffic) to the airport and administered the oath. Mrs. Kennedy, wearing a blood-stained suit and a dazed expression on her face, stood next to the new president to witness the transfer of power.

Mrs. Kennedy spent the rest of the trip in the back of the plane with her husband's coffin. When someone asked if she would like to change out of the stained clothes, she said no: "Let them see what they've done."

Three thousand people waited in the darkness for Air Force One to return to Andrews Air Force Base, just outside Washington. After the plane landed, the dead president's brother, Attorney General Robert F. Kennedy, rushed up the steps. With Mrs. Kennedy, he accompanied the body to Bethesda Naval Hospital for an autopsy.

After they left, President Johnson came down different steps and spoke briefly before television cameras and microphones that had been set up.

■ Stunned, Mrs. Kennedy witnessed the transfer of power to Lyndon Johnson.

"This is a sad time for all people," he said. "We have suffered a loss that cannot be weighed. For me it is a deep personal tragedy. I know the world shares the sorrow that Mrs. Kennedy and her family bear. I will do my best. That is all I can do. I ask for your help—and God's."

The nonstop television coverage continued. All across the country, people stayed home and watched sad scenes in Washington and mysterious events in Dallas.

They saw black limousines pull up in front of the White House. President Kennedy's body lay in a closed coffin in the East Room of the White House, then was taken to the rotunda of the U.S. Capitol. The line of people waiting to see his casket stretched forty blocks, with people standing four abreast.

Meanwhile in Dallas, police questioned Oswald for twelve hours over a two-day period. Remarkably, no one took notes or taped the sessions. Oswald told police—and reporters at a news conference—he had not killed the president.

Police were convinced he was guilty, though. They invited more than forty reporters (some with television cameras) to witness Oswald's transfer to a more secure prison on the morning of November 24.

The TV cameras were rolling—and millions of people were watching at home—when the handcuffed Oswald stepped off an elevator and started walking through the crowded basement of the police headquarters. Suddenly a nightclub owner named Jack Ruby broke through the crowd, with a .38-caliber revolver aimed at Oswald.

He shot Oswald in the stomach, shouting, "You killed my president, you rat!"

Several policemen jumped on Ruby. "I am Jack Ruby," he said. "You all know me."

And they did. Many of the police were regulars at Ruby's club.

■ Jack Ruby shot Lee Harvey Oswald while millions watched on TV.

He was taken straight upstairs to an interrogation room. "I hope I killed the son of a bitch," Ruby said. "It will save you guys a lot of trouble."

Downstairs, Oswald gurgled but never spoke. He was rushed to Parkland Hospital, to the same emergency room that had treated President Kennedy and Governor Connally two days before. Within ten minutes, the doctors had Oswald on the operating table. But it was too late; he died at 1:07 P.M.

Back at the police station, Ruby was proud of what he had done but insisted he hadn't planned the shooting. He said he'd seen the smirk on Oswald's face and just pulled out the pistol he often carried.

People who knew Ruby agreed he hadn't planned the shooting. The reason: He left his beloved dog Sheba in the car while he went into the police headquarters, and they said he would have made sure Sheba was well taken care of if he thought he might not return.

Ruby marveled at his luck in shooting Oswald. "If I had planned this, I couldn't have had my timing better," he told police. "It was one chance in a million." He said he was glad Oswald's death meant Mrs. Kennedy wouldn't have to return to Dallas for a trial: Now she wouldn't have to "go through this ordeal for this son of a bitch."

Mrs. Kennedy was going through another ordeal: her husband's funeral. She decided she wanted him buried in Arlington National Cemetery, just across the Potomac River from Washington. She planned a dignified funeral, beginning with a solemn procession from the Capitol to St. Matthew's Cathedral.

With a long black veil covering her face, Mrs. Kennedy walked with her husband's brothers, Robert and Edward Kennedy. Behind them came princes, presidents, Supreme Court justices, congressmen, and leaders from all over the world. (Mrs. Kennedy wanted to continue on foot all the way to Arlington after the funeral mass, but she was warned that would be too much for some of the old men following her.)

Television cameras covered the mass at St. Matthew's Cathedral. When the coffin was carried out of St. Matthew's, the cameras

■ Mrs. Kennedy and her husband's brothers, Robert *(left)* and Edward, led a procession from the White House to St. Matthew's Cathedral.

showed John Fitzgerald Kennedy, Jr., saluting his father's casket. It was young John's third birthday.

Following Mrs. Kennedy's wishes, the president was buried in Arlington Cemetery. Mrs. Kennedy lit a torch—known as the eternal flame—that is still burning today at his grave.

Little Patrick and another Kennedy baby who had been born dead were buried next to their father. And after her death in 1994, Mrs. Kennedy was buried beside them.

In Texas, Lee Harvey Oswald's mother asked that her son be buried in Arlington, too. But Oswald's brother, Robert, said, "Oh, shut up, Mother."

In 1964, Jack Ruby was convicted of murder and sentenced to death. While in prison, he tried to kill himself three times. The Texas Court of Criminal Appeals reversed the conviction (because

■ Mrs. Kennedy and her children, Caroline and John, Jr., watched the casket leave St. Matthew's Cathedral.

of errors made in his trial) and ordered a new trial. By then, though, Ruby was sick with cancer. He died at Parkland Hospital in 1967.

For more than thirty years people have argued about who shot President Kennedy. A week after the assassination, President Johnson asked Supreme Court Chief Justice Earl Warren to lead a commission that would investigate John Kennedy's death. The president asked the Warren Commission to complete the investigation quickly, before the 1964 presidential election.

The Warren Commission interviewed ninety-four witnesses. Its staff members questioned another 395 people, and sixty-one people—including President and Mrs. Johnson—were allowed to send sworn statements. The commission delivered a report to the White House on September 24, 1964.

In the report, the commission said Lee Harvey Oswald, acting alone, had fired three shots from the sixth floor of the Texas School Book Depository. The first shot had missed, according to the commission, but the second bullet was amazing: It had entered Kennedy's upper back, gone out the front of his neck (near his tie knot), entered Connally's right shoulder, exited his chest, went through his wrist, snapped a bone, and finally stopped in the governor's thigh.

The third shot had shattered John Kennedy's skull.

At first Americans were relieved to have answers to their questions about the assassination. But as time went by, more and more people began to doubt those answers.

They wondered how that second bullet—which came to be known as "the magic bullet"— could have traveled so far and done so much damage. Many people believed at least one more shot must have been fired by at least one more gunman.

In the late 1960s a New Orleans district attorney, Jim Garrison, thought he had uncovered a conspiracy behind the assassination. In 1969 he charged a New Orleans businessman, Clay Shaw, with conspiracy to kill the president of the United States. But the evidence against Shaw was not convincing. After a trial that lasted more than five weeks, the jury took forty-five minutes to find him not guilty.

Still, so many people continued to doubt the Warren Commission report that the House of Representatives decided to reopen the investigation in 1978. The House Select Committee on Assassinations interviewed witnesses and listened to a tape, supposedly from Dallas Police Officer H. B. McClain's dictabelt on Dealey Plaza, that seemed to record four separate gunshots. The committee decided that someone else, probably on the grassy knoll across from the Texas School Book Depository, had also fired at least one shot at the motorcade.

After the committee released its report, McClain stepped forward to say the recording was not from his dictabelt, but from another one somewhere else in Dallas.

Still, many people—70 percent of all Americans, according to one survey in the early 1990s—believed someone else had been involved in the death of John Kennedy.

But who?

Some people think the Cuban government hired Oswald (and maybe someone else) to kill the president; others think the Soviet government, organized crime, or even the U.S. Central Intelligency Agency were behind the conspiracy. (In 1992, a movie titled *JFK* even implied Lyndon Johnson himself was involved.)

With all of these possible killers, some people began to wonder whether Oswald had fired *any* shots. Someone could have set up the sniper's nest just to make Oswald *look* guilty, they reasoned.

Studying the Kennedy assassination—and trading theories about it—has become a consuming hobby for some people; for others, it has become a profitable business. Several Dealey Plaza witnesses regularly give speeches and sign autographs. A few have changed their stories considerably over the years.

So the mystery continues. Some people think Oswald was part of a conspiracy to kill the president, others think he acted alone, and others are convinced he was innocent.

Still others, perhaps, have no idea what happened but enjoy guessing.

After the shock of President Kennedy's death, many people worried about what might happen next. What if someone *had* killed Lyndon Johnson that day—or what if something happened to him now? Who would become president?

According to the Presidential Succession Act of 1896, the

speaker of the House of Representatives would assume the presidential duties.

The House speaker in 1963 was a seventy-two-year-old congressman named John McCormack, who had served in Congress since 1928. Many people worried he was too old and too fragile to take on the duties of the presidency. What if *he* died?

The Presidential Succession Act outlined a long list of potential people to take over the presidency if the speaker died. But the worriers were not satisfied. They did not want the presidency passing from one old man to the next. They wanted stability in the White House.

So Congress proposed the Twenty-fifth Amendment to the Constitution, which allows the president to appoint a new vice president when the office is vacant. The new amendment became law in 1967 after two-thirds of the states approved it.

Congress also passed a law making an attack on the President a federal crime. And the Secret Service, devastated by the assassination, redoubled its efforts to protect the president. Presidents no longer rode in open limousines. Manhole covers were welded shut along parade routes; newspaper racks and trash baskets were removed. And agents closed their ranks even more tightly around the president.

It has been said that America lost its innocence on November 22, 1963. One thing is sure: America changed the way it thought about Jack Kennedy.

People who had once criticized him—as too Catholic, too brash, too liberal—suddenly began to speak of him as a beloved leader. More than thirty years later, politicians still imitate his style, his humor, even his haircut.

The Kennedy family has continued to fascinate the public. Americans have watched, copied, and criticized the Kennedys in a way that makes some people say we treat them like royalty.

In the years right after President Kennedy's death, many Americans expected his brothers—especially Robert—to take his place in the White House. Robert Kennedy did run for president in 1968, but he was shot in a hotel kitchen after winning the California Democratic primary. He died the next day.

Several civil rights leaders were also assassinated in the 1960s: Medgar Evers, Malcolm X, and Martin Luther King, Jr. Those who spoke of lost innocence said John Kennedy's death had set off a decade of turmoil: the assassinations, the Vietnam War, the war protests, the riots and other deaths that accompanied the civil rights movement.

But much of this turmoil had already begun before President Kennedy's death. (Evers, for instance, was shot a few months before the president.) America was changing in the 1960s, and not even Camelot could stop it.

Gerald Ford

Ronald Reagan

"Honey, I forgot to duck."
PRESIDENT RONALD REAGAN (TO HIS WIFE)

Still Keeping the President Safe

IN THE YEARS since John Kennedy's death, the security around the president has grown constantly tighter. But the danger has also increased. On three occasions the president has faced a loaded gun.

The first two incidents happened in September 1975. Until then, every attack on a president had been made by a man. Then two different women pulled a gun on President Gerald R. Ford within seventeen days of each other.

On September 5, 1975, President Ford was shaking hands with

■ Secret Service agents hustled President Ford into the California Statehouse
after Lynette Fromme pointed a gun at him.

people outside the California state capitol building in Sacramento. Suddenly he saw a pistol, two feet away, pointed directly at him. Secret Service agent Larry Buendorf, moving through the crowd with the president, also saw the gun. He knocked it away and tackled the young woman who had been holding it.

Other agents also jumped on her. "It didn't go off, fellas!" she cried.

The agents found the gun had four bullets in it, but none in the firing chamber.

Agents hustled President Ford into the statehouse, where he gave a speech, as planned, on violent crime. He did not mention the gun that had just been pointed at him.

Meanwhile, police learned the young woman was Lynette Alice Fromme (but everyone called her Squeaky). She was a follower of mass murderer Charles Manson, who had led a group of people (but not, apparently, Fromme) in killing a Hollywood actress and her friends a few years before.

Fromme said she didn't like the way President Ford was running the country. "Well, you know," she told a jailer, "when people around you treat you like a child and pay no attention to things you say, you have to do something."

Worried Secret Service agents begged President Ford to cut back on his travels. (It is always harder to protect the president when he leaves the White House.) But President Ford was getting ready for the 1976 presidential campaign, and he wanted as many people as possible to see him. He often spent sixteen or eighteen hours a day speaking to people and shaking their hands. He refused to change his schedule.

"I have no intention of allowing the government of the people to be held hostage at the point of a gun," the president said. He agreed, though, to wear a bulletproof vest.

But the vest was uncomfortable, and President Ford didn't always wear it. He wasn't wearing it, for instance, when he was leaving the St. Francis Hotel in San Francisco almost three weeks later, on September 22. A woman across the street pulled a .38-caliber pistol out of her purse. She aimed and fired.

The bullet whizzed over the president's head, ricocheted off a car, and hit a cab driver in the groin. A man standing next to the woman—a former Marine named Oliver Sipple—knocked her hand so she couldn't fire again. Secret Service agents jumped on her.

Other agents shoved President Ford into his limousine, pushed

■ President Ford winced as Sara Jane Moore fired a gun at him.

him onto the floor of the car, and piled on top of him. The car sped to the airport. Just seventeen minutes after the shooting, Air Force One took off, with the president safely on board.

Agents identified the shooter as Sara Jane Moore, a forty-six-year-old woman who used to be a police informant. She said she didn't know why she shot at the president. Then she wondered who would pick up her nine-year-old son after school.

The police found someone else to pick up the boy. Someone else had to raise him, too. Twenty years later, Sara Jane Moore and Squeaky Fromme were still in prison: They were both convicted, under the federal law passed after President Kennedy's death, of attempted assassination of the president of the United States, and they were both sentenced to life imprisonment.

Gerald Ford lost the presidential race that year to a former peanut farmer named Jimmy Carter. Four years later, President Carter lost the 1980 election to a former actor named Ronald Reagan.

Ronald Reagan had been in more than fifty movies. His political fans remembered his heroic roles in *Knute Rockne, All American* and *Kings Row.* His opponents remembered he had costarred with a chimpanzee in *Bedtime for Bonzo.*

But after March 30, 1981, people began to talk about another movie in connection with Ronald Reagan. The movie was *Taxi Driver,* which—even though President Reagan had never even seen it—turned out to be one of the most important movies of his life.

Taxi Driver tells the story of a lonely cab driver named Travis

Bickle, who stalks a political candidate, shoots some criminals, and rescues a runaway girl named Iris.

In 1976 a disturbed young man watched *Taxi Driver* at least sixteen times in darkened Los Angeles movie theatres. The young man's name was John Hinckley, Jr., but he began to think of himself as Travis Bickle. And he fell in love with Iris—or the actress Jodie Foster, who had played Iris and was now a freshman at Yale University. Hinckley visited Yale, called Jodie Foster, and left notes for her; but he never met her.

The young actress received other fan letters, too, but something about John Hinckley's letters worried her. She didn't answer them, and she gave them to her dean.

Hinckley grew more desperate to gain her attention. Like Travis, he began to stalk a political leader. His first target was President Jimmy Carter; Hinckley followed President Carter to Dayton, Ohio, and to Nashville, Tennessee, where he was arrested when his guns set off a metal detector at the airport.

He came within shooting distance of President Carter a couple of times, but Hinckley couldn't bring himself to pull the trigger. After the 1980 election, he switched his attention to Ronald Reagan.

Hinckley went to Washington twice and mingled with crowds waiting to see the new president. When Ronald Reagan appeared, though, Hinckley found he still couldn't pull the trigger.

He sent more letters to Jodie Foster, who still didn't reply. When he called her on the telephone (and recorded their conversations), she told him, "I can't carry on these conversations with people I don't know."

Hinckley set out to make sure she would know who he was. On March 24, 1981, he left his parents' home in Colorado to fly to Los Angeles. Then, one day later, he started a four-day bus trip that he hoped would take him to Yale.

He planned to find Jodie Foster and shoot her. Or maybe he would just shoot himself in front of her.

But somewhere along the way he learned his ticket wouldn't take him to Yale. His bus was going to Washington, D.C.

He arrived in Washington at 5:30 A.M. on Sunday, March 29. He thought about leaving right away for Yale, but he was tired of riding on buses. He checked into a hotel, which happened to be across the street from the Secret Service headquarters. He planned to stay just a day or two before continuing his trip.

But shortly before noon the next day, he came across a copy of President Reagan's schedule in the *Washington Star*. It showed the president was expected to give a speech at the Washington Hilton at one-forty that afternoon.

Hinckley decided to stay in Washington. He took a shower, got dressed, and loaded his .22-caliber revolver with six Devastator bullets, designed to explode on contact.

Then he sat down at the desk in his room and wrote a letter to Jodie Foster. He told her again how much he loved her. Then he wrote:

. . . I just cannot wait any longer to impress you. I've got to do something now to make you understand in no uncertain terms that I am doing all of this for your sake. By sacrificing my freedom and possibly my life, I hope to change your mind about me. This letter is being written an hour before I leave for the Hilton Hotel.

Jodie, I am asking you to please look into your heart and at least give me a chance with this historical deed to gain your respect and love.

I love you forever.

John Hinckley

He left the letter in his room and went downstairs to catch a cab to the Washington Hilton. At the hotel, Hinckley waited outside with other people hoping to catch a glimpse of Ronald Reagan.

After the president finished his speech, several reporters came running out of the hotel. "Press! Press!" they shouted. "Let us through!"

They stepped in front of people who had been waiting, but Hinckley held on to his spot. "No," he told the reporters. "We were here first."

President Reagan came out of the hotel at 2:25 P.M., smiling and waving to the people on the sidewalk. A reporter called out a question, and the president's press secretary, James Brady, went over to answer.

Suddenly Hinckley dropped into a combat crouch position and

■ This series of photographs shows President Reagan's reaction to the gunfire. Although he didn't realize it yet, he had been shot.

■ The scene in front of the Washington Hilton just a few moments after the shooting

stretched out both arms to aim his revolver at the president. He fired six shots within nine seconds.

The first bullet hit Brady in the forehead. The second hit Washington Metropolitan Police Officer Thomas Delahanty in the neck. Secret Service Agent Timothy J. McCarthy threw himself between Hinckley and the president, and took the third bullet in the chest.

The fourth and sixth bullets didn't hit anyone, but the fifth ricocheted off the limousine and into President Reagan's chest—although nobody (not even the president) knew it at the time.

Secret Service agent Jerry Parr shoved the president onto the floor of the limousine and covered him with his body. Parr ordered the driver to take off, and the limousine sped toward the White House.

Hinckley kept pulling the trigger even after his revolver was empty. Secret Service agents, police officers, and bystanders

■ Police arrested John Hinckley, Jr., immediately.

jumped on Hinckley. One of the bystanders tried to choke Hinckley, and a Secret Service agent had to strike the man in order to rescue Hinckley. Then the agents and police shoved Hinckley into a police cruiser.

President Reagan was still on the floor of the limousine, protected by agent Parr, when he felt a sharp pain in his chest. The president told Parr to get off.

When Parr got off, he saw a little blood trickling out of the corner of the president's mouth. Then President Reagan coughed up some blood. Afraid he might have broken the president's ribs when he jumped on him, Parr told the driver to go to nearby George Washington University Hospital.

(Doctors later said Parr's decision probably saved the president's life. President Reagan was losing blood—internally—so rapidly that they did not think he could have survived the trip to the White House.)

The pain was getting worse and President Reagan was having trouble breathing, but he insisted on walking into the hospital by himself. The moment he stepped inside the doors, though, his knees buckled and he fell to the floor.

The president's face was gray, and the emergency room workers thought at first he was having a heart attack. But when they stripped off his shirt, a nurse found the bullet hole.

The bullet had punctured his left lung, and his chest was filling with blood. Doctors suctioned out three and a half quarts of blood, replaced it with transfusions, and prepared the president for surgery.

Surgeons found the bullet and removed it, just an inch from President Reagan's heart.

News of the attack frightened many Americans, who remembered it was time for the Twenty-Year Curse to kill another president. But President Reagan did not die—even though his injury was probably more serious than James Garfield's or William McKinley's. Modern surgery, transfusions, X rays, and antibiotics made the president's recovery almost certain.

It reassured many people to hear that President Reagan was joking about his injury. When his wife arrived at the hospital, the president said, "Honey, I forgot to duck." When everyone fussed over him in the recovery room, he wrote a note—he couldn't talk because of the tubes in his throat—saying, "If I'd had this much attention in Hollywood, I'd have stayed there."

McCarthy and Delahanty also recovered fairly smoothly. Doctors removed the bullet from McCarthy's chest but decided to leave the bullet in Delahanty's neck rather than risk causing a spinal cord injury. But when they learned the bullet was a Devastator, which could explode, they decided to remove it. Two volunteer surgeons worked alone on Delahanty. They carefully removed the bullet—which did not explode—and Delahanty continued his recovery.

Only one of the Devastator bullets from Hinckley's gun exploded. That one was in James Brady's brain.

■ President Reagan and his wife, Nancy, returning to the White House after his hospital stay

Brain tissue was oozing out of Brady's head when he arrived at George Washington University Hospital. Doctors doubted he would survive. About three hours after the shooting, the television networks reported Brady's death.

But they were wrong; Brady survived—through several operations and years of rehabilitation. His brain was permanently damaged, and his left side was paralyzed. He learned to walk with a cane but used a wheelchair most of the time.

John Hinckley was charged with the attempted assassination of the president of the United States. After a forty-two-day trial, the jury found him not guilty by reason of insanity. Many people were outraged: It was obvious that Hinckley had shot President Reagan, Brady, and the others. How could he be considered not guilty?

His lawyers and parents agreed the phrase *not guilty* was misleading. They preferred to say he was *not responsible* for his actions because of his mental illness. (Fifteen years later he was still confined to St. Elizabeth's Hospital for the mentally ill in Washington.)

Many Americans were still outraged. Politicians talked about eliminating "not guilty by reason of insanity" as a defense. Others talked about requiring a death sentence for anyone attempting to kill the president of the United States.

When Hinckley heard about that, he said, "That wouldn't have stopped me."

His father asked what *would* have stopped him.

"Maybe if I'd had to wait awhile to buy a gun," he said. "Had to fill out forms, or get a permit first, or sign in with the police, or anything complicated. I probably wouldn't have done it."

More than a year after the shooting, a California group asked Jim Brady's wife, Sarah, to help campaign for stricter gun control laws in that state. Mrs. Brady said she wanted to help, but she didn't want to embarrass President Reagan, who opposed gun control.

But something happened in 1984 that changed her mind. The Bradys were visiting Jim's hometown in Centralia, Illinois, when their five-year-old son, Scott, picked up what looked like a toy pistol on the front seat of a friend's pickup truck. The toy turned out to be a real gun, fully loaded.

Scott did not hurt himself—or anyone else—but Sarah Brady knew she could no longer remain silent. She joined Handgun Control, Inc., and began campaigning for tougher gun control laws.

In 1994 President Bill Clinton signed the Brady Bill, which requires a five-day waiting period for anyone who wants to buy a gun. Police are supposed to use those five days to check the buyer's background. The Brady Law supporters hope the waiting period will save some of the 20,000 Americans who are killed by handguns every year.

They also hope John Hinckley, Jr., was right: Maybe the paperwork will stop the next person who wanted to buy a gun to kill the president.

But the threats and attacks on presidents have not stopped. On

October 29, 1994, Francisco Martin Duran fired a semiautomatic weapon at the White House while President Clinton was inside, watching a football game on television. Wrestled to the ground by tourists, Duran was convicted of attempted assassination and sentenced to forty years in prison.

Attacks like Duran's show why Secret Service agents must be vigilant. They must check the places the president visits, the food he eats, the visitors he sees, the mail he receives, even the bathrooms he uses. Worried about the possibility of a car or truck bomb exploding on Pennsylvania Avenue, the Secret Service closed the street to traffic in front of the White House in 1995.

But despite these precautions, the president of the United States continues to live in danger. And he—or she—always will.

If You Want to Learn More...

Nothing stuns a country like the death of its leader. On the four occasions when American presidents were killed—and on the seven other occasions when presidents were attacked—most of the nation's businesses stopped. Everyone's eyes turned to the president and his family.

The one business that always kept going was the news business. Reporters tried to cover every aspect of the attack. How did it happen? Who did it? Why? How is the president? And his family?

You can see for yourself what reporters found out—and sometimes the mistakes they made—if you look in old newspapers. Many libraries have microfilm copies of the *New York Times,* the *Washington Post,* and regional newspapers. (The coverage of the attack usually begins the day after the shooting.) In addition, weekly newsmagazines—*Time, Newsweek,* and *U.S. News & World Report*—provide records of the attacks since the 1930s.

Many books have also been written about the assassinations. Author Gerald Posner says more than 2,000 books have been written about the death of President Kennedy alone. Shortly after the assassination, Mrs. Kennedy and others taped interviews with William Manchester for *The Death of a President;* they also provided information to the Warren Commission, which published a twenty-six-volume report in 1964. Posner's own book, *Case Closed: Lee Harvey Oswald and the Assassination of JFK,* describes many of the conspiracy theories that developed after Kennedy's death.

Lincoln's death also prompted a lot of books. In *Lincoln: A Photobiography*, Russell Freedman writes, "More books have been written about Abraham Lincoln than any other American." For an hourly account of the assassination day, see *The Day Lincoln Was Shot* by Jim Bishop. For a discussion of the conspiracies and earlier attempts on Lincoln's life, see *The Lincoln Murder Conspiracies* by William Hanchett and *Beware the People Weeping: Public Opinion and the Assassination of Abraham Lincoln* by Thomas Reed Turner.

Not as much has been written about the deaths of James Garfield and William McKinley. *The Trial of the Assassin Guiteau: Psychiatry and Law in the Gilded Age* by Charles E. Rosenberg and the last couple of chapters in *Garfield's Orbit* by Margaret Leech and Harry Brown describe the events that led to President Garfield's death. Margaret Leech also wrote the prizewinning *In the Days of McKinley*, which ends with a detailed description of that president's final days.

Biographies of Andrew Jackson, Franklin Roosevelt, Harry Truman, Gerald Ford, and Ronald Reagan usually contain information about the attempts on those presidents' lives. In addition, you'll find interesting information in *The Times of My Life* by Betty Ford with Chris Chase; *Thumbs Up: The Life and Courageous Comeback of White House Press Secretary Jim Brady* by Mollie Dickensen; *Breaking Points* by Jack and JoAnn Hinckley with Elizabeth Sherrill; and *My Turn* by Nancy Reagan with William Novak.

You can also learn more about the assassinations by visiting the locations where they occurred. Ford's Theatre in Washington, D.C., and the Texas School Book Depository in Dallas, Texas, are particularly interesting. The Theodore Roosevelt Inauguration National Historic Site in Buffalo, New York, displays items related to the death of William McKinley, but nothing marks the site where James Garfield was shot. The old Sixth and B Street Depot was torn down in 1907, and the National Gallery of Art now stands in its place.

Index

Page numbers in *italics* refer to illustrations.